Vegetarian

Bloomsbury Books
London

This edition published 1994 by Bloomsbury Books,
an imprint of The Godfrey Cave Group,
42 Bloomsbury Street, London, WC1B 3QJ.

ISBN 1 85471 557 7

Printed and bound in Great Britain.

Vegetarian

Contents

Courgette Tian

Serves 4

Working time: about 45 minutes

Total time: about 1 hour and 15 minutes

Calories 190
Protein 8g
Cholesterol 100mg
Total fat 9g
Saturated fat 3g
Sodium 195mg

750 g	courgettes, trimmed and finely sliced	1¼ lb	2	small eggs, beaten	2
3 tsp	virgin olive oil	3 tsp	2 tbsp	freshly grated Parmesan cheese	2 tbsp
60 g	brown rice	2 oz	1 tbsp	shredded fresh rocket leaves	1 tbsp
1	garlic clove	1	1 tbsp	shredded fresh basil leaves	1 tbsp
¼ tsp	salt	¼ tsp	1 tbsp	finely chopped flat-leaf parsley	1 tbsp
3	shallots, finely chopped	3	⅛ tsp	white pepper	⅛ tsp

Place the courgettes in a heavy-bottomed saucepan with 2 teaspoons of oil and cook them gently over low heat, covered, until they are just tender – about 10 minutes. Stir from time to time to prevent the courgettes from sticking.

Meanwhile, rinse the brown rice under cold running water and place it in a small, heavy-bottomed saucepan with 30 cl (½ pint) of water. Bring to the boil, then reduce the heat, cover the pan and simmer for 15 minutes. Drain the rice well and set it aside, covered.

Preheat the oven to 180°C (350°F or Mark 4). Crush the garlic with the salt. Heat the remaining teaspoon of oil in a small, heavy-bottomed saucepan, add the shallots and garlic, and soften them over very low heat, covered, for about 5 minutes.

Lightly grease a wide, shallow gratin dish. In a large mixing bowl, stir together the courgettes, rice, shallots and garlic; add the eggs and half of the Parmesan. Stir well, then mix in the rocket, basil, parsley and pepper. Transfer the mixture to the prepared dish, levelling the courgette slices so that they lie flat, and sprinkle on the remaining Parmesan.

Bake the tian in the oven, uncovered, for 20 minutes, then increase the oven temperature to 220°C (425°F or Mark 7) and bake it for a further 10 to 15 minutes, until a crust has formed. Serve hot or warm.

Spanish Omelette

Serves 4

Working time: about 20 minutes

Total time: about 35 minutes

Calories
190
Protein
7g
Cholesterol
110mg
Total fat
10g
Saturated fat
2g
Sodium
260mg

2 tbsp	virgin olive oil	**2 tbsp**
1	onion, chopped	**1**
2	garlic cloves, chopped	**2**
2	small courgettes (about 125 g/4 oz), trimmed and thinly sliced	**2**
2	eggs	**2**
2	egg whites	**2**
½ tsp	salt	**½ tsp**
	freshly ground black pepper	
1	large potato (about 300 g/10 oz), peeled, cooked in boiling water	**1**
	for 25 to 30 minutes, drained and coarsely chopped	
125 g	French beans, trimmed, cooked in boiling water for 5 minutes, drained, refreshed under cold running water and cut into 2.5 cm (1 inch) lengths	**4 oz**
2	tomatoes (about 175 g/6 oz), skinned, seeded and chopped	**2**
½ tbsp	chopped fresh oregano, or ½ tsp dried oregano	**½ tbsp**

Heat 1½ tablespoons of the oil in a heavy frying pan over medium heat. Add the onion and fry until it is soft – about 3 minutes. Add the garlic and courgettes, cover the pan and cook the vegetables gently for 10 minutes, stirring them occasionally. Remove the pan from the heat.

In a large bowl, beat together the eggs and egg whites, the salt and some black pepper. Add the fried vegetables, the potato, beans, tomatoes and oregano, and stir gently to mix the ingredients.

Heat the remaining oil in a 25 cm (10 inch) non-stick frying pan and pour in the egg mixture. Cook the omelette gently over medium heat for 3 to 4 minutes, until the underside is pale golden. Place the frying pan under a preheated medium-hot grill and cook the omelette for a further 2 to 3 minutes, or until it is lightly set. Cut into quarters and serve.

Ratatouille Terrine

Serves 4

Working time: about 1 hour

Total time: about 4 hours and 30 minutes (includes chilling)

Calories 120
Protein 3g
Cholesterol 0mg
Total fat 8g
Saturated fat 1g
Sodium 10mg

250 g	aubergine, diced	**8 oz**
2 tsp	salt	**2 tsp**
350 g	courgettes, trimmed	**12 oz**
2 tbsp	virgin olive oil	**2 tbsp**
150 g	onion, coarsely chopped	**5 oz**
150 g	sweet red pepper, seeded, deribbed and coarsely chopped	**5 oz**
150 g	sweet green pepper, seeded, deribbed and coarsely chopped	**5 oz**
1 tsp	dried oregano or marjoram	**1 tsp**
½ tsp	ground coriander	**½ tsp**
1 tbsp	tomato paste	**1 tbsp**
250 g	tomatoes, skinned, seeded and coarsely chopped	**8 oz**
1½ tbsp	agar flakes	**1½ tbsp**
	freshly ground black pepper	

In a bowl, toss the aubergine with the salt. Place the aubergine in a colander and weight it down with a small plate. Let it drain for 30 minutes, then rinse it under cold running water to rid it of the salt. Drain it well.

Slice the courgettes lengthwise; chop and reserve any uneven pieces and trimmings. Blanch the strips in boiling salted water for 3 minutes, refresh them under cold running water. Drain them well.

Line a 22 by 10 by 7.5 cm (9 by 4 by 3 inch) loaf tin with plasticizer-free film. Lay two strips of courgette lengthwise down the centre of the tin, then line the long sides with remaining strips, placing one end of each strip on the centre seam

of courgettes and overlapping the strips slightly.

Heat the olive oil in a saucepan and add the onion, sweet peppers and courgette trimmings. Cover the pan and soften the vegetables over gentle heat for 6 to 8 minutes. Add the aubergine, oregano, coriander and tomato paste, stir well and cook for a further 25 minutes. Stir in the tomatoes and agar flakes and simmer for a further 5 minutes. Season with some black pepper. Pour into the lined tin and smooth the top. Allow to cool, then chill for at least 3 hours.

Trim the courgette slices level with the rim of the tin, turn the terrine on to a plate. Slice with a serrated knife.

Aubergine and Mozzarella Ramekins

Serves 6

Working time: about 1 hour and 30 minutes

Total time: about 2 hours

Calories 275

Protein 19g

Cholesterol 35mg

Total fat 13g

Saturated fat 6g

Sodium 385mg

3	large aubergines (each 500 g/1 lb), sliced to 5 mm (¼ inch rounds)	**3**
1 tsp	salt	**1 tsp**
2 tbsp	virgin olive oil	**2 tbsp**
350 g	low-fat mozzarella cheese, grated	**12 oz**
2 tbsp	chopped fresh oregano	**2 tbsp**
100 g	thick Greek yogurt	**3½ oz**
15 cl	plain low-fat yogurt	**¼ pint**
1 tbsp	cut chives	**1 tbsp**

	Tomato Coulis	
750 g	ripe tomatoes, skinned, seeded and chopped, or 400 g (14 oz) can tomatoes, with juice, chopped	**1½ lb**
1	carrot, finely chopped	**1**
1	small onion, finely chopped	**1**
1	stick celery, trimmed, finely chopped	**1**
1	bay leaf	**1**
1	red chili pepper, seeded, finely chopped	**1**
¼ tsp	salt	**¼ tsp**

For the tomato coulis, place all the ingredients in a pan with 8 cl (3 fl oz) of water. Boil, reduce to low, cover, simmer for 45 mins. Discard the bay leaf and process for 2 mins. Strain back into the pan and keep it warm.

While the coulis is cooking, arrange the aubergine slices on a wire rack over a tray, and sprinkle with ½ tsp of salt. Drain for 15 minutes, then turn over and repeat. Finally, rinse them well under cold running water. Pat them dry on paper towels.

Preheat the oven to 190°C (375°F or Mark 5). Lightly grease six ramekins.

Brush the slices on one side with oil. Grill the oiled sides under high heat for 3 to 4 mins, until lightly coloured. Line the bottom of each ramekin with 2 or 3 slices of aubergine, grilled side down, sprinkle on a little mozzarella and oregano. Add layers of aubergine, mozzarella and oregano until the ramekins are full, finishing with a layer of aubergine.

Bake in the oven for 20 mins. Process the yogurts and chives in a blender for 1 min, until smooth.

Remove from the oven and stand for 2 to 3 mins. Carefully run a knife round each one and invert the contents on to serving plates. Serve with the coulis and yogurt sauce.

Aubergine Rolls with a Ricotta-Raisin Filling

Serves 4		Calories 270
Working time: about 45 minutes		Protein 14g
		Cholesterol 15mg
Total time: about 1 hour and 15 minutes		Total fat 13g
		Saturated fat 5g
		Sodium 275mg

4	aubergines (each 250 g/8 oz)	**4**
2 tsp	virgin olive oil	**2 tsp**
250 g	low-fat ricotta cheese	**8 oz**
60 g	raisins, chopped	**2 oz**
30 g	pine-nuts, toasted	**1 oz**
2 tbsp	freshly grated Parmesan cheese	**2 tbsp**
¼ tsp	salt	**¼ tsp**

	freshly ground black pepper	
60 g	sun-dried tomatoes, soaked for 10 mins in 15 cl (¼ pint) boiling water	**2 oz**
1 tbsp	balsamic, or red wine vinegar	**1 tbsp**
2 tbsp	fresh wholemeal breadcrumbs	**2 tbsp**
1 tsp	arrowroot	**1 tsp**
2 tbsp	tomato paste	**2 tbsp**

Preheat the oven to 220°C (425°F or Mark 7). Oil a large baking sheet.

Trim both ends of aubergines. Remove a wide strip of skin from both sides of each, then cut them lengthwise into 6, with a border of skin at the sides. Lay the slices on the sheet. Brush with olive oil. Cover loosely with foil and roast in the oven for about 10 mins, to soften. Remove from the oven and reduce the oven temperature to 180°C (350°F or Mark 4).

Beat the ricotta with the raisins, pine-nuts, half the Parmesan, salt and pepper. Stir in the tomatoes, drained and chopped. Reserve tomato liquid.

Lay the aubergine slices flat and place a heaped tsp of the filling on one end of each. Roll up the slices. Pack all 24 rolls into a shallow baking dish.

Blend the vinegar with 2 tbsp of the reserved tomato liquid and pour round the rolls. Sprinkle the rolls with the breadcrumbs and Parmesan, and black pepper. Cover with foil and bake for 30 mins, until tender. Remove from the oven and spoon the juices into a jug. Cover, and set in a warm place.

Make up the cooking juices to 30 cl (½ pint) with the reserved tomato liquid and water. Dissolve the arrowroot in 2 tbsp of this mixture, then stir it into the jug. Pour into a saucepan and bring to the boil, stirring, then simmer for a few seconds until clear and thick. Remove from the heat, stir in the tomato paste and pour over the rolls. Crisp the dish under a hot grill before serving.

Aubergine Fans

Serves 4

Working time: about 45 minutes

Total time: about 3 hours

Calories 275

Protein 20g

Cholesterol 60mg

Total fat 14g

Saturated fat 6g

Sodium 350mg

4	aubergines (each 250 g/8 oz), washed and dried	**4**
4	garlic cloves, quartered lengthwise	**4**
4	large, firm beef tomatoes, cut lengthwise into 1 cm (½ inch) slices	**4**
175 g	low-fat mozzarella cheese, cut into thin slices	**6 oz**
	freshly ground black pepper	
60 g	fine fresh wholemeal breadcrumbs	**2 oz**

1	small egg, beaten	**1**
1 tbsp	grated Parmesan cheese	**1 tbsp**
	Basil Spread	
30 g	basil leaves, very finely chopped	**1 oz**
1 tbsp	extra virgin olive oil	**1 tbsp**
60 g	thick Greek yogurt	**2 oz**
1 tbsp	grated Parmesan cheese	**1 tbsp**
½ tsp	dry mustard	**½ tsp**

Preheat the oven to 180°C (350°F or Mark 4).

Cut the stems off the aubergines. Slice lengthwise from near the stem end of each, making cuts 1 cm (½ inch) apart and leaving the slices joined by 3 to 4 cm (1¼ to 1½ inches) at the stem end. Make 4 small cuts into the unsliced stem ends. Press a slice of garlic into each cut.

Mix the basil with the oil in a basin. Add yogurt, Parmesan and mustard, and stir until evenly mixed. Divide among aubergines, a little over each cut surface.

Sprinkle the tomato and mozzarella with plenty of black pepper. Place a slice or two of each between the segments of aubergine. Cut any remaining tomato and mozzarella into smaller pieces and insert where there is a space to fill.

Put the 4 aubergines in a dish, packed close. Oil the base of the dish, and sprinkle with 1 to 2 tsps of the breadcrumbs. Brush a little beaten egg over the aubergine, sprinkle on the remaining breadcrumbs, pressing down lightly to keep them in place. Press down on the upper surface of each to fan out the slices, and sprinkle with Parmesan.

Cover with foil, and bake for 2 to 2½ hours. Remove foil, increase the oven temperature to maximum and cook for 10 to 15 mins, until the topping is crisp.

12

Pumpkin Soufflé

Serves 4

Working time: about 30 minutes

Total time: about 2 hours and 45 minutes

Calories 200
Protein 11g
Cholesterol 85mg
Total fat 12g
Saturated fat 6g
Sodium 300mg

750 g	slice of pumpkin, seeds removed	1½ lb	1	egg yolk	1
2 tbsp	dry breadcrumbs	2 tbsp	¼ tsp	salt	¼ tsp
30 g	unsalted butter	1 oz	1 tsp	ground cinnamon	1 tsp
2 tbsp	plain flour	2 tbsp	3 tbsp	freshly grated Parmesan cheese	3 tbsp
12.5 cl	skimmed milk	4 fl oz	5	egg whites	5

Preheat the oven to 190°C (375°C or Mark 5).

Wrap the pumpkin in a sheet of foil and place it on a baking sheet. Bake it in the oven for about 1 hour, until it is soft. Check the pumpkin after this time; if it is still hard, return it to the oven for a further 20 minutes to cook it through. When the pumpkin is ready, remove it from the oven and set it aside to cool, uncovered.

Meanwhile, grease a 90 cl (1½ pint) soufflé dish and dust the base and sides with the breadcrumbs. Reduce the oven temperature to 200°C (400°F or Mark 6).

Using a metal spoon, scoop all the pumpkin pulp from the skin and pass the pulp through a nylon sieve; there should be about 350 g (12 oz) of sieved pumpkin. Put in a saucepan and, stirring continuously, dry out the pulp over medium heat until it becomes fairly dense and is no longer wet – about 10 minutes. Set aside.

In a small saucepan, melt the butter over gentle heat. Remove the pan from the heat. Using a wooden spoon, stir in the flour, then stir in the milk a little at a time. Return the pan to the heat and cook the mixture for about 30 seconds, stirring, until it thickens. Take the pan off the heat again and stir in the egg yolk, followed by the pumpkin, salt, cinnamon and 2 tablespoons of the Parmesan. Set the mixture aside.

Whisk the egg whites until they hold their shape, fold them gently into the pumpkin mixture. Turn the mixture into the prepared soufflé dish and sprinkle it with the remaining Parmesan.

Bake the souffle in the oven for about 40 minutes, until it is well risen and set. Serve.

Asparagus Mousse with Goat Cheese Sauce

Serves 4

Working
time: about
30 minutes

Total time:
about
1 hour and
40 minutes

Calories
195

Protein
17g

Cholesterol
90mg

Total fat
10g

Saturated fat
5g

Sodium
470mg

750 g	asparagus, trimmed and peeled	1½ lb	1	egg yolk		
15 g	unsalted butter	½ oz	3	egg whites		
1	onion, chopped	1		flat-leaf parsley sprigs, for garnish		
2 tsp	cornflour	2 tsp		**Goat Cheese sauce**		
15 cl	skimmed milk	¼ pint	1 tsp	cornflour	1 tsp	
¼ tsp	salt	¼ tsp	4 tbsp	white wine	4 tbsp	
	freshly ground black pepper		1	garlic clove, crushed		
¼ tsp	freshly grated nutmeg	¼ tsp		freshly ground black pepper		
1 tbsp	chopped flat-leaf parsley	1 tbsp	125 g	soft goat cheese, cubed	4 o	

Preheat the oven to 180°C (350°F or Mark 4).

Cut off the asparagus tips about 1 cm (½ inch) below the buds, and cut the stalks in half. Cook stalks in boiling water for 2 mins. Add the tips and cook for 1 min, drain and refresh under cold running water. Halve the tips lengthwise and reserve.

Melt the butter. Add the onion, cover, cook over high heat for 3 mins, stirring occasionally, until soft. Blend the cornflour with 2 tbsp of the milk. Stir in the remaining milk, add to the pan with the salt, some pepper and the nutmeg. Bring to the boil, cook, stirring, for 2 mins, to form a sauce.

Process the asparagus stalks, onion sauce, parsley,

egg yolks and whites for 1 min, until smooth. Turn into 4 greased ramekins. Cover with greased foil and place in a baking dish with 1 cm (½ inch) boiling water. Bake for about 1 hr or until mousse is just firm.

In a pan blend the cornflour with a little of the wine. Stir in the remaining wine, garlic and some pepper. Bring to the boil, stirring, remove from the heat and stir in the cheese until it melts. Keep the sauce warm.

Remove cooked mousses from water. Leave to stand for 10 mins, then loosen from moulds with a knife and invert onto warm plate. Spoon on sauce, garnish with asparagus tips and serve.

Fennel Baked in a Roquefort Sauce

Serves 4

Working time: about 35 minutes

Total time: about 1 hour

Calories 165
Protein 113g
Cholesterol 10mg
Total fat 8g
Saturated fat 3g
Sodium 530mg

4	fennel bulbs, (about 200 g/ 7 oz each), trimmed halved lengthwise	**4**
175 g	low-fat cottage cheese	**6 oz**
60 g	Roquefort cheese	**2 oz**
	freshly ground black pepper	
30 g	fresh wholemeal breadcrumbs	**1 oz**
1 tsp	safflower oil	**1 tsp**
30 g	watercress leaves	**1 oz**
1 tsp	cornflour	**1 tsp**
12.5 cl	skimmed milk	**4 fl oz**
1 tbsp	dry vermouth	**1 tbsp**

Blanch the fennel bulbs in a large saucepan of boiling water for about 5 minutes, until the layers have separated and softened lightly. Drain and set them aside.

Press the cottage cheese through a nylon sieve into a bowl. Crumble the Roquefort into the bowl, add some black pepper, and beat well. In another bowl, blend the breadcrumbs with the oil.

Preheat the oven to 180°C (350°F or Mark 4). Open out the layers of the halved fennel bulbs. Set one third of the cheese mixture aside in a separate bowl. Spread each layer of one of the halved fennel bulbs with some of the remaining cheese mixture and tuck in a few of the watercress leaves. Repeat with the other bulbs, cut sides down, in each of four individual gratin dishes, or place all the fennel in a large, shallow ovenproof dish.

In a small saucepan, blend the cornflour with 3 tablespoons of the milk. Add the remaining milk, then cook over medium heat, whisking continuously, until the sauce has thickened slightly. Remove the pan from the heat and stir in the vermouth and the reserved cheese mixture. Spoon the sauce over the fennel and sprinkle on the oiled breadcrumbs.

Bake the fennel in the oven for about 20 minutes, until the breadcrumbs are golden, and serve hot.

Chicory Baked with Pistachio-Stuffed Tomatoes

Serves 4

Working time: about 30 minutes

Total time: about 45 minutes

Calories 200

Protein 9g

Cholesterol 10mg

Total fat 14g

Saturated fat 3g

Sodium 90mg

4	chicory heads (each 125 g/4 oz)	**4**
8	firm small tomatoes	**8**
1 tbsp	virgin olive oil	**1 tbsp**
60 g	shelled pistachio nuts, skinned and coarsely chopped	**2 oz**
3	garlic cloves, finely chopped	**3**
15 g	dry wholemeal breadcrumbs	**½ oz**
30 g	Parmesan cheese, grated	**1 oz**
1	lemon, cut into wedges, for garnish	**1**

Preheat the oven to 220°C (425°F or Mark 7).

Trim the chicory and slice each head lengthwise into four. Blanch the cut chicory in boiling water for 30 seconds. Drain and refresh the chicory under cold running water, and set it aside. Slice off and discard the tops of the tomatoes. Using a teaspoon, hollow out and discard the insides of the tomatoes, then turn them upside down on paper towels to drain.

Heat the olive oil in a frying pan and sauté the pistachio nuts for 2 minutes, until crisp. Add the garlic and sauté for another 1 to 2 minutes, until the garlic has softened. Remove the pan from the heat.

Lay the chicory slices in diagonal lines acroos the base of a rectangular baking dish, alternating these with lines of hollowed-out tomatoes.

Fill the tomatoes with the garlic and pistachio mixture, spooning any extra neatly round them in the dish. Brush the olive oil from the frying pan over the chicory. Mix the breadcrumbs with the Parmesan cheese and sprinkle this mixture over the chicory. Bake for 15 minutes, or until the chicory and tomatoes are tender.

Serve hot, garnished with the lemon wedges.

Suggested accompaniment: crusty bread.

Editor's Note: To skin pistachio nuts, drop them into boiling water and simmer them for 1 minute. Drain them thoroughly, wrap them in a towel and rub them briskly until they have shed their skins.

Spicy Mould of Courgettes, Cabbage and Leeks

Serves 6

Working time: about 30 minutes

Total time: about 14 hours and 30 minutes (includes chilling)

Calories 295

Protein 5g

Cholesterol 0mg

Total fat 10g

Saturated fat 2g

Sodium 220mg

500 g	courgettes, trimmed and coarsely grated	**1 lb**
500 g	Savoy cabbage, trimmed and very finely shredded	**1 lb**
500 g	leeks, trimmed, washed to remove all grit, sliced into very fine rings	**1 lb**
¾ tsp	salt	**¾ tsp**
4 tbsp	virgin olive oil	**4 tbsp**
5 cm	piece fresh ginger root, grated	**2 inch**
1	dried hot red chili pepper, crushed	**1**
2	garlic cloves, crushed	**2**
1 tbsp	coriander seeds, crushed	**1 tbsp**
2 tsp	curry powder	**2 tsp**
1 tbsp	low-sodium soy sauce or shoyu	**1 tbsp**
5	sheets nori seaweed, each about 20 cm (8 inches) square	**5**

Place the courgettes, cabbage and leeks in separate bowls. Sprinkle ¼ tsp of salt over each and leave to drain for 1 hour, to rid them of bitter juices. After this, squeeze out each very thoroughly in a piece of muslin. Place them back in separate bowls.

Heat 2 tbsp of the oil in a frying pan over medium heat. Add the ginger, chili and garlic to the pan and stir-fry for about 1 minute. Pour over the leeks and toss in the flavoured oil. Heat the remaining 2 tbsp of oil in a clean pan and fry the coriander and curry powder for 1 minute. Pour the spiced oil over the cabbage and toss it thoroughly. Leave both bowls for 1 hour.

In a large, square shallow dish, mix the soy sauce with 2 tbsp of water. Moisten the sheets of nori in the solution and leave in the dish for 5mins, then remove and cut each diagonally into two triangles. Lay out the triangles facing the same way. Line a 1.25 litre (2 pint) bowl with the triangles, placing them in the bowl one at a time and overlapping them; one 45° corner should be placed in the bottom and the other should overhang the rim.

Press the cabbage mixture down in the bottom of the bowl. Follow with the courgettes, then the leeks. Fold over the overhanging nori. Set a small plate on top of the mould and place a weight on top. Refrigerate for at least 12 hours.

To serve, turn out, and slice into wedges.

Lacy Pancakes with a Spinach Filling

Serves 4	
Working time: about 45 minutes	
Total time: about 1 hour	

Calories 410	
Protein 18	
Cholesterol 25mg	
Total fat 16g	
Saturated fat 5g	
Sodium 360mg	

1 kg	spinach, washed and stemmed	**2 lb**	
15 g	unsalted butter	**½ oz**	
1	onion, chopped	**1**	
2	garlic cloves, crushed	**2**	
1	sweet red pepper, seeded, deribbed and cut into 2.5 cm (1 inch) strips	**1**	
300 g	potatoes, peeled and grated	**10 oz**	
	freshly ground black pepper		
125 g	rice flour	**4 oz**	
⅛ tsp	salt	**⅛ tsp**	
2	egg whites, made up to 30 cl (½ pint) with water	**2**	
2 tbsp	safflower oil	**2 tbsp**	
125 g	low-fat mozzarella cheese, thinly sliced	**4 oz**	

Blanch the spinach in boiling water for 1 min, drain and refresh under cold water. Drain again, squeeze dry and chop.

Melt the butter in a frying pan over low heat. Add the onion and garlic and cook for 2 minutes. Mix in the pepper strips and potatoes, cook, stirring, for 20 minutes, until the potatoes are cooked through. Remove from the heat and stir in the spinach and some black pepper. Cover and set it aside.

Put the flour and salt into a bowl and gradually beat in the egg whites and water to make a batter. Heat a 15 cm (6 inch) crêpe pan or frying pan over medium-high heat, then spread a little oil over the entire surface of the pan with a paper towel. Pour in about 2 tbsp of batter and immediately swirl the pan to coat the bottom with a thin, even layer. Cook until it is firm – about 1 minute – then turn over. Cook the second side until dry – about 30 secs. Slide on to a plate. Make 7 more pancakes, spreading oil over the pan as necessary. Stack the cooked pancakes on top of one another.

Preheat the oven to 190°C (375°F or Mark 5). Lay each pancake in turn out flat and spoon an eighth of the spinach mixture down the centre. Roll up the pancake, then transfer it to an oiled, shallow dish. Lay the cheese slices evenly on top and bake for about 15 minutes, until the cheese has melted. Serve at once.

Spinach, Stilton and Tomato Roulade

Serves 4

Working time: about 40 minutes

Total time: about 55 minutes

Calories 200
Protein 18g
Cholesterol 115mg
Total fat 10g
Saturated fat 5g
Sodium 410mg

500 g	spinach, washed, stems removed	**1 lb**
2	egg yolks	**2**
¼ tsp	grated nutmeg	**¼ tsp**
30 g	fresh wholemeal breadcrumbs	**1 oz**
¼ tsp	salt	**¼ tsp**
	freshly ground black pepper	
4	egg whites	**4**

Stilton and Tomato Filling		
175 g	low-fat soft cheese	**6 oz**
45 g	Stilton cheese, rind removed, mashed	**1½ oz**
2 tbsp	finely cut chives	**2 tbsp**
4	tomatoes, skinned, seeded and chopped	**4**
	freshly ground black pepper	

Preheat the oven to 200°C (400°F or Mark 6). Line the bottom and sides of a 30 by 20 cm (12 by 8 inch) Swiss roll tin with parchment paper.

Boil the spinach for 2 to 3 minutes, until wilted. Drain in a colander, refresh under cold water, place in a piece of muslin and squeeze out all the liquid. Purée in a food processor.

Stir together the puréed spinach, the egg yolks, nutmeg, breadcrumbs, salt and some black pepper. Whisk the egg whites until they are fairly stiff. Using a metal tablespoon, fold 1 tbsp of the whites into the spinach mixture, then carefully fold in the remainder. Spread the mixture evenly in the prepared Swiss roll tin and

smooth the surface. Bake for 10 to 15 minutes, until firm to the touch, remove from the oven, cover with a clean towel and set aside to cool.

Blend the soft cheese and the mashed Stilton together in a bowl. Mix in the cut chives, chopped tomatoes and some freshly ground black pepper. Turn the spinach rectangle out on to a sheet of greaseproof paper and carefully peel off the lining paper. Spread the filling over the surface. Starting from one of the short sides, roll the base and filling into a cylinder: lift one end of the underlying greaseproof paper to start the roulade off, and nudge it along by gradually lifting the rest of the paper. Slice and serve.

Spinach and Pine-Nut Layered Terrine

Serves 4

Working time: about 45 minutes

Total time: about 1 hour and 40 minutes

Calories 295
Protein 25g
Cholesterol 75mg
Total fat 13g
Saturated fat 5g
Sodium 530mg

1 kg	spinach, washed, stems removed	**2½ lb**
175 g	low-fat ricotta cheese	**6 oz**
60 g	low-fat cottage cheese	**2 oz**
30 g	Parmesan cheese, freshly grated	**1 oz**
30 g	pine-nuts, toasted	**1 oz**
1	egg, separated	**1**
1	egg white	**1**
	freshly ground black pepper	

	Red Pepper Sauce	
2	sweet red peppers, seeded, deribbed and sliced	**2**
1	onion, sliced	**1**
2	garlic cloves, crushed	**2**
¼ litre	unsalted vegetable stock	**8 fl oz**
60 g	fresh wholemeal breadcrumbs	**2 oz**
⅛ tsp	salt	**⅛ tsp**
	freshly ground black pepper	

Blanch 12 spinach leaves in boiling water for 30 secs. Drain and refresh under cold water. Drain again and lay out on paper towels. Place the remaining spinach, washed, still wet in the pan. Cover and cook gently until wilted and reduced by ⅓ – 2 to 3 mins. Drain, squeeze out in muslin, and chop.

Preheat the oven to 200°C (400°F or Mark 6).

Line a 1 litre (1¾ pt) terrine mould with the blanched spinach, leaving enough overhanging to fold over the top. Mix the cheeses with the pine-nuts and the egg yolk. Whisk the egg whites until stiff but not dry, then fold them into the spinach. Layer the mould with ⅓ of the

spinach mixture, then ½ of the cheese mixture; continue alternatively, finishing with spinach; smooth each layer before the next. Fold the spinach leaves over the top. Cover with buttered greaseproof paper, place in a deep dish with water ⅔ of the way up the sides. Bake until firm to touch – about 45 mins.

Bring peppers, onion, garlic and stock to the boil, then simmer, covered, to soften vegetables (20 mins). Add breadcrumbs and seasoning. Purée.

Remove terrine from oven and rest it. Reheat the sauce. Turn out terrine onto warmed dish. Serve sliced, with the sauce.

Stuffed Mushroom Caps

Serves 6

Working time: about 35 minutes

Total time: about 1 hour and 10 minutes

Calories 185
Protein 7g
Cholesterol 15mg
Total fat 6g
Saturated fat 3g
Sodium 260mg

6	large field, or open cup, mushrooms, wiped clean, stalks removed and finely chopped	6
½ tsp	salt	½ tsp
	freshly ground black pepper	
1 tbsp	virgin olive oil	1 tbsp
1	onion, finely chopped	1
1	small sweet red pepper, seeded, deribbed and finely chopped	1
125 g	Italian round-grain rice	4 oz
2	garlic cloves, crushed	2
30 g	pine-nuts	1 oz
35 cl	unsalted vegetable stock	12 fl oz
2 tbsp	shredded fresh basil leaves	2 tbsp
125 g	low-fat mozzarella cheese, diced	4 oz
30 g	fresh wholemeal breadcrumbs	1 oz
1 tbsp	chopped parsley	1 tbsp

Preheat the oven to 200°C (400°F or Mark 6).

Place the mushroom caps in a shallow dish with 2 tbsps of cold water. Season with a little of the salt and some freshly ground black pepper. Cover with a lid or foil, and set aside.

Heat the oil in a large, heavy-bottomed saucepan over medium heat. Add the onion and red pepper and cook gently for 6 to 8 minutes, until soft. Stir in the chopped mushroom stalks, the rice, garlic and pine-nuts, and cook for 5 minutes, stirring occasionally, until the rice is very lightly browned. Add the stock, basil, the remaining salt, and some pepper. Bring to the boil, then reduce the heat and cover the pan tightly. Cook gently for 20 to 25 minutes, until the rice is cooked and the stock has been absorbed. Meanwhile, cook the mushrooms in the oven for 20 minutes, until almost soft.

Remove the rice mixture from the heat and stir in the diced mozzarella cheese, then divide the mixture evenly among the mushrooms, mounding it neatly on top of each one. Sprinkle on the breadcrumbs and return to the oven for another 10 minutes, or until the mozzarella cheese begins to melt. Serve the mushrooms sprinkled with the chopped parsley.

Scorzonera with Pepper and Onion Relish

Serves 6

Working (and total) time: about 45 minutes

Calories
190
Protein
7g
Cholesterol
0mg
Total fat
5g
Saturated fat
1g
Sodium
140mg

1 kg	scorzonera, scrubbed well	**2¼ lb**
1	large sweet red pepper, seeded, deribbed and coarsely chopped	**1**
9	pickled mild green chili peppers, finely chopped	**9**
1	red onion, finely chopped	**1**
6	spring onions, trimmed, white bottoms sliced, green tops coarsely sliced	**6**
4	tomatoes, skinned and seeded, finely chopped	**4**

½	cucumber, peeled and diced	**½**
1½ tbsp	capers	**1½ tbsp**
6 tbsp	coarsely chopped flat-leaf parsley	**6 tbsp**
1 tbsp	virgin olive oil	**1 tbsp**
1	lime, juice only	**1**
⅛ tsp	cayenne pepper	**⅛ tsp**
3	black olives, stoned and sliced	**3**
	lamb's lettuce, for garnish	

Peel the scorzonera with a vegetable peeler and trim both ends. Drop them into acidulated water as you work, to prevent discoloration. Drain the scorzonera and put them in a large, heavy-bottomed saucepan. Add sufficient water to cover the roots and bring them to the boil. Cook over high heat for 10 to 20 minutes, depending on the thickness of the scorzonera, until tender. Test the roots with the point of a sharp knife.

While the scorzonera is cooking, prepare the relish. Place all the remaining ingredients except the lambs's lettuce in a large bowl and combine them thoroughly.

Drain the scorzonera in a colander, arrange them on a hot serving dish and garnish with the lamb's lettuce. Spoon the relish over the roots and serve.

Suggested Accompaniment: granary bread.

Editor's Note: salsify may be used instead of scorzonera.

Sweet Potato Timbales with Two Paprika Sauces

Serves 6	**Calories** 140
Working time: about 1 hour	**Protein** 5g
	Cholesterol 10mg
Total time: about 2 hours and 45 minutes (includes chilling)	**Total fat** 5g
	Saturated fat 2g
	Sodium 185mg

500 g	sweet potatoes, peeled and cut into chunks	**1 lb**
2 tbsp	double cream, chilled	**2 tbsp**
4	egg whites, chilled	**4**
1 tsp	finely cut chives, plus a few whole chives for garnish	**1 tsp**
1 tsp	virgin olive oil	**1 tsp**

3	sweet red peppers, (about 500 g/1 lb) seeded, deribbed and finely sliced	**3**
1	onion, thinly sliced	**1**
750 g	tomatoes, roughly chopped	**1½ lb**
1 tsp	paprika	**1 tsp**
½ tsp	salt	**½ tsp**
	freshly ground black pepper	
2 tbsp	fromage frais	**2 tbsp**

Boil the potatoes in water until soft – 20-25 mins. Drain, cool for about 30 mins, then chill for 1 hour.

Line 6 ramekins with parchment paper; leave lining round the side proud of the rim by 1 cm (½ inch).

Preheat the oven to 180°C (350°F or Mark 4).

Put the potatoes and cream into a processor, purée until smooth, transfer to a bowl. In another bowl, whisk the egg whites until they form soft peaks. Using a metal spoon, fold the egg whites gently into the potato, then add the chives. Divide among the ramekins, smoothing the tops. Arrange in a baking dish with water ⅔ of the way up the sides, and cover with parchment paper.

Bake the timbales for 30 mins, or until risen, puffy and just firm.

Heat the oil gently in a frying pan, and sweat the peppers and onion for 5 mins. Add the tomatoes and bring to the boil; cover and simmer for 15 mins. Add the paprika and simmer, covered, for a further 5 mins. Remove from the heat. When it has cooled, add seasoning, and purée the mixture. Sieve the purée into a bowl, then divide between two pans. Add the *fromage frais* to one, stir through, and warm both pans gently. Unmould the timbales onto plates, garnish with whole chives and a spoonful of each sauce.

Potato, Carrot and Celeriac Rösti

Serves 4

Working time: about 40 minutes

Total time: about 1 hour and 10 minutes

Calories 200
Protein 3g
Cholesterol 25mg
Total fat 9g
Saturated fat 5g
Sodium 165mg

500 g	potatoes, scrubbed	1 lb	¼ tsp	salt	¼ tsp
250 g	carrots, peeled	8 oz		freshly ground black pepper	
300 g	celeriac, peeled	10 oz	45 g	unsalted butter	1½ oz

Cook the potatoes, in their skins, in a saucepan of boiling water for 6 minutes, then drain them well. Carefully peel the potatoes while they are still hot. Allow to cool for 10 minutes, then chill them for 20 minutes.

Using a vegetable grater or mouli julienne machine, coarsely shred the potatoes, carrots and celeriac. Place the shredded vegetables in a large mixing bowl. season them with the salt and with black pepper to taste, and mix them well together.

Heat half of the butter in a large non-stick frying pan until it begins to bubble. Reduce the heat to low and add the *rösti* mixture, pressing it down gently with a spatula to form a flat cake.

Cook for about 10 minutes, until the *rösti* is golden-brown underneath, shaking the pan gently now and then to prevent sticking.

Place a large flat plate on top of the frying pan, remove it from the heat and carefully invert the *rösti* on to the plate. Return the frying pan to the heat, add the remaining butter and heat it until it is bubbling hot. Slide the *rösti* back into the pan and cook the second side for 5 to 6 minutes, until golden-brown. Turn the *rösti* on to a hot plate and serve immediately.

Suggested accompaniment: salad of red and white cabbage with chopped parsley, tossed in a vinaigrette dressing.

Baked Potatoes with an Onion and Chive Filling

Serves 4

Working time: about 20 minutes

Total time: about 2 hours

Calories 270
Protein 7g
Cholesterol 3mg
Total fat 3g
Saturated fat 1g
Sodium 245mg

2	large potatoes (about 500 g/1 lb each), scrubbed and pricked	**2**
2	Spanish onions, unpeeled, halved lengthwise	**2**
250 g	thick Greek yogurt	**8 oz**
2 tbsp	finely cut chives	**2 tbsp**
½ tsp	salt	**½ tsp**
	freshly ground black pepper	

Preheat the oven to 200°C (400°F or Mark 6).

Place the potatoes and the onion halves on a rack in the middle of the oven and bake them until they are soft when pierced with a skewer; the onions will take about 45 minutes and the potatoes will need about 1½ hours. Do not turn off the oven at the end of this time.

When the onions are cooked, remove them from the oven. Allow them to cool a little, then peel them. Remove and reserve the centres of the onions and roughly chop the remainder.

Cut the cooked potatoes in half lengthwise. Using a spoon, scoop the flesh into a bowl, leaving a 1 cm (½ inch) thick potato shell. Mash the potato flesh, then mix in the yogurt, chives, salt and some black pepper.

Half fill the shells with the mashed potato mixture. Add a layer of chopped roast onion, and top the onion with the rest of the potato mixture. Garnish each potato half with the reserved onion centre. Return the stuffed potatoes to the oven for about 15 minutes, to heat them through.

Suggested accompaniment: radish and watercress salad.

Curried Swede Soup

<table>
<tr><td>Serves 4</td></tr>
<tr><td>Working time: about 20 minutes</td></tr>
<tr><td>Total time: about 1 hour</td></tr>
</table>

Calories	185
Protein	4g
Cholesterol	0mg
Total fat	7g
Saturated fat	2g
Sodium	425mg

1 tbsp	safflower oil	1 tbsp
1	onion (about 125 g/4 oz), chopped	1
350 g	swedes, cut into 5 mm (¼ inch) dice	12 oz
175 g	parsnips, cut into 5 mm (¼ inch) dice	6 oz
1	small sweet red pepper, seeded, deribbed and cut into 5 mm (¼ inch) dice	1
1	small cooking apple (about 90 g/3 oz), cut into 5 mm (¼ inch) dice	1
30 g	brown basmati rice	1 oz

½ tsp	medium-hot curry powder	½ tsp
½ tsp	ground coriander	½ tsp
¼ tsp	ground cumin	¼ tsp
⅛ tsp	ground turmeric	⅛ tsp
⅛ tsp	ground ginger	⅛ tsp
1	garlic clove, crushed	1
30 cl	tomato juice	½ pint
½ tsp	salt	½ tsp
90 cl	unsalted vegetable stock	1½ pints
15 g	sultanas	½ oz
15 g	desicated coconut, toasted	½ oz

Heat the oil in a large, heavy-bottomed saucepan or fireproof casserole and sweat the onion, swedes and parsnips over medium heat for 5 minutes. Add the red pepper and cook for a further 2 to 3 minutes, stirring occasionally. Then add the apple, rice, spices and garlic and cook, stirring constantly, for 2 minutes. Finally, mix the salt, tomato juice, stock and sultanas and bring the mixture to the boil. Reduce the heat to

a simmer, cover the pan, and cook the soup for 30 minutes. Just before serving, stir in the coconut.

Suggested accompaniment: sourdough rye bread.

Editor's Note: To toast desiccated coconut, spread the coconut out on a baking sheet and place it in a 180°C (350°F or Mark 4) oven for 10 minutes, stirring it once.

Stir-Fried Vegetables in a Sweet-and-Sour Sauce

Serves 4

Working
(and total)
time: about
30 minutes

Calories
240

Protein
9g

Cholesterol
0mg

Total fat
13g

Saturated fat
2g

Sodium
30mg

1¼ tbsp	safflower oil	1¼ tbsp
350 g	baby sweetcorn, trimmed if necessary, halved lengthwise	12 oz
1	large sweet red pepper, seeded, deribbed and cut into strips	1
350 g	young carrots, trimmed and thinly sliced diagonally	12 oz
350 g	bean sprouts	12 oz
350 g	mange-tout, strings removed	12 oz
2 tsp	dark sesame oil	2 tsp
	freshly ground black pepper	

Sweet-and-Sour Sauce

3 tsp	arrowroot	3 tsp
30 cl	unsweetened pineapple juice	½ pint
2 tbsp	low-sodium soy sauce or shoyu	2 tbsp
1 tbsp	freshly grated ginger root	1 tbsp
1	garlic clove, crushed	1
15 cl	unsalted vegetable stock	¼ pint
1 tsp	clear honey	1 tsp
5	spring onions, trimmed and finely sliced	5

To make the sauce, place the arrowroot in a medium-sized saucepan and gradually blend in the pineapple juice. Stir in the soy sauce or shoyu, grated ginger, garlic, vegetable stock, honey and spring onions. Bring to the boil, reduce the heat, and simmer for 5 minutes, stirring frequently. Set the sauce aside.

Heat the safflower oil in a wok or large, heavy frying pan over high heat. Add the sweetcorn, red pepper and carrots, and stir-fry them for 4 minutes. Add the bean sprouts and mange-tout, and stir-fry for a further 1 to 2 minutes, until cooked but still slightly crunchy.

Add the sweet-and-sour sauce to the wok. Reduce the heat and cook the mixture for 1 to 2 minutes more, still stirring, to warm sauce through.

Season with the sesame oil and with some freshly ground black pepper. Serve immediately.

Suggested accompaniment: white or brown rice.

Creamy Coconut Curry

Serves 4		**Calories** 170
Working time: about 45 minutes		**Protein** 5g
		Cholesterol 10mg
Total time: about 1 hour		**Total fat** 9g
		Saturated fat 2g
		Sodium 330mg

15 g	ghee or unsalted butter	**½ oz**
1	onion, finely chopped	**1**
1½ tsp	ground turmeric	**1½ tsp**
2 tsp	ground coriander	**2 tsp**
1 tsp	ground fenugreek	**1 tsp**
2 tsp	black mustard seeds	**2 tsp**
350 g	carrots, coarsely chopped and blanched for 30 seconds in boiling water	**12 oz**
1	small cauliflower (about 750 g/ 1½ lb), boken into florets and blanched for 30 seconds in boiling water	**1**

½ tsp	salt	**½ tsp**
175 g	French beans, topped and tailed, cut in half and blanched for 30 seconds in boiling water	**6 oz**
60 g	raisins	**2 oz**
8	small hot green chili peppers, seeded and finely chopped	**8**
3	small bananas, peeled and diced	**3**
60 g	creamed coconut, grated	**2 oz**
½	lemon, juice only	**½**
1 tbsp	chopped fresh mint	**1 tbsp**
1 tbsp	chopped fresh coriander leaves freshly ground black pepper	**1 tbsp**

Melt the ghee in a large, saucepan over medium heat. Add the onion and fry it, stirring frequently, until it is transparent – about 3 minutes. Stir in the turmeric, ground coriander, fenugreek and black mustard seeds, and fry the spices with the onion for about 2 mins. Then mix in the carrots and cauliflower, and the salt. Reduce the heat to low, cover, and cook for 5 mins. Add the beans, re-cover the pan and cook for a further 3 mins. Stir in 30 cl (½ pint) of water, then lightly stir in the raisins and half the chilies. Bring to the boil, cover again, lower the heat and simmer for 10 mins, or until the carrots are tender.

Mix in the bananas and coconut, and simmer, uncovered, for 3 mins. Add the lemon juice, mint, chopped coriander, remaining chilies and some freshly ground black pepper. If the curry seems dry, add a little extra water. Simmer for 2 mins more and serve.

Mexican Sweet Potato Stew

Serves 4

Working time: about 40 minutes

Total time: about 1 hour and 10 minutes

Calories
270

Protein
7g

Cholesterol
0mg

Total fat
9g

Saturated fat
1g

Sodium
150mg

600 g	sweet potatoes, cut into large chunks	**1¼ lb**
350 g	slice of pumpkin, seeded and chopped	**12 oz**
2 tbsp	safflower oil	**2 tbsp**
1	onion, finely chopped	**1**
2	garlic cloves, crushed	**2**
½ tsp	chili powder	**½ tsp**
250 g	okra, topped, tailed and chopped	**8 oz**
1	sweet green pepper, seeded, deribbed and chopped	**1**
4	fresh hot red chili peppers, seeded and finely chopped	**4**
175 g	fresh or frozen sweetcorn kernels	**6 oz**
400 g	canned tomatoes, with their juice	**14 oz**
5	cloves	**5**
30 cl	unsalted vegetable stock	**½ pint**
2 tbsp	tomato paste	**2 tbsp**
⅛ tsp	salt	**⅛ tsp**
	freshly ground black pepper	

Put the potatoes in a saucepan, cover them with water and bring to the boil. Cover the pan, reduce the heat and simmer the potatoes until they are tender – about 10 minutes. Remove and set aside. Put the pumpkin into the same cooking water and bring it to the boil. Reduce the heat, cover the pan again and simmer until it , too, is tender – 5 to 7 minutes. Drain the pumpkin and set it aside.

Heat the oil in a large, heavy-bottomed saucepan and sauté the onion and garlic over very gentle heat for about 7 minutes, or until the onion is tender. Add the chili powder, okra, sweet pepper, chili peppers, sweetcorn, tomatoes and their juice, cloves and stock. Bring the mixture to the boil, then reduce the heat and cook over medium-low heat for about 10 minutes, or until the liquid has reduced and thickened. Add the tomato paste, potatoes, pumpkin, salt and some black pepper and stir gently. Cover and simmer the stew for a further 10 minutes. Serve it hot.

Suggested accompaniments: tacos or tortillas; green salad.

Hot and Sour Potato and Turnip Casserole

Serves 4

Working time: about 45 minutes

Total time: about 1 hour and 20 minutes

Calories 270
Protein 7g
Cholesterol 0mg
Total fat 12g
Saturated fat 3g
Sodium 265mg

1 tsp	coriander seeds	1 tsp
1 tsp	black peppercorns	1 tsp
5	cardamom pods	5
4	cloves	4
1½ tbsp	safflower oil	1½ tbsp
1	small onion, finely chopped	1
2	garlic cloves, crushed	2
1 tsp	freshly grated ginger root	1 tsp
1	fresh or dried red chili pepper, halved lengthwise and seeded	1
500 g	potatoes, diced	1 lb
250 g	turnips, diced	8 oz

250 g	French beans, topped and tailed, in 2.5 cm (1 inch) lengths	8 oz
5 or 6	fresh curry leaves (optional)	5 or 6
½ tsp	salt	½ tsp
500 g	tomatoes, skinned, seeded, and chopped	1 lb
1½ tbsp	fresh lemon juice	1½ tbsp
2 tsp	sugar	2 tsp
150 g	thick Greek yogurt or 15 cl (¼ pint) soured cream	5 oz
3 tbsp	chopped fresh coriander	3 tbsp
2 tsp	ground turmeric	2 tsp

Toast the coriander seeds, peppercorns, cardamom pods and cloves in a dry frying pan over medium heat for 1 minute. Grind finely, either in coffee grinder or in a mortar with a pestle.

Heat the oil over medium heat in a large saucepan. Fry the onion, garlic, ginger, ground spices and chili for 5 mins, stirring frequently. Add the potatoes, turnips, beans, curry leaves, and salt. Stir well, cover, and sweat the vegetables for 10 mins, stirring occasionally.

Blend the tomatoes until smooth, and add to the

casserole. Simmer until the potatoes are almost done – about 15 mins. Stir in 15 cl (¼ pint) of water, cook for 5 mins, stir in another 15 cl (¼ pint) and cook for 5 mins more. Remove from the heat and mix in the lemon juice and 1 tsp of the sugar. Discard the curry leaves, and the chili pepper.

Mix the yogurt with the remaining sugar and the tumeric. Stir half of the yogurt mixture into the casserole. Pour the rest into the centre of the casserole, sprinkle over the chopped coriander and serve.

Avocado, Flageolets, Almonds and Brown Rice

125 g	dried flageolet beans, picked over	**4 oz**
250 g	brown rice	**8 oz**
¼ tsp	salt	**¼ tsp**
1	small ripe avocado	**1**
1	lemon, juice only, strained	**1**
60 g	blanched and skinned almonds, toasted	**2 oz**
6 tbsp	chopped parsley	**6 tbsp**
2 tbsp	chopped fresh wild fennel	**2 tbsp**
4 tbsp	plain low-fat yogurt	**4 tbsp**
1 tbsp	virgin olive oil	**1 tbsp**
1 tsp	Dijon mustard	**1 tsp**
1	garlic clove, crushed	**1**
1	large lettuce, leaves washed and dried, for garnish	**1**

Rinse the beans under cold water, then put them into a large pan, with enough cold water to cover them by about 7.5 cm (3 inches). Discard any beans that float to the surface. Cover, leaving the lid ajar, and slowly bring to the boil. Boil for 2 minutes, then turn off the heat, soak the beans, covered, for at least 1 hour.

Rinse the beans, place them in a pan, and pour in enough water to cover them by about 7.5 cm (3 inches). Boil for 10 minutes, then drain and rinse again. Wash the pan, replace the beans and add enough water to cover them again by about 7.5 cm (3 inches). Bring to the boil, then reduce the heat to a strong simmer and cook, covered, until tender – about 1 hour. If they appear to be

drying out, pour in hot water. Drain, rinse, and set aside to cool for about 30 minutes.

Bring 2 litres (3½ pints) of water to the boil in a pan. Stir in the rice and salt, reduce the heat and simmer, uncovered, until the rice is tender – about 40 minutes. Drain, rinse, drain and cool thoroughly.

Halve, stone, peel and chop the avocado and coat the pieces in half of the lemon juice. In a large bowl, mix the avocado, almonds, parsley and fennel with the beans and rice. Beat the yogurt, olive oil, mustard, garlic and remaining lemon juice. Fold this into the rice salad.

Serve the salad in a bowl lined with lettuce.

Caribbean Spiced Rice

Serves 4

Working (and total) time: about 50 minutes

Calories 540

Protein 9g

Cholesterol 0mg

Total fat 6g

Saturated fat 2g

Sodium 250mg

350 g	basmati rice	**12 oz**
1 tsp	ground allspice	**1 tsp**
½ tsp	salt	**½ tsp**
2	garlic cloves, sliced	**2**
	freshly ground black pepper	
90 cl	unsalted vegetable stock	**1½ pints**
2	green bananas	**2**
1 tbsp	white wine vinegar	**1 tbsp**
1	small carrot, finely chopped	**1**
¼	sweet red pepper, finely chopped	**¼**
1	stick celery, finely chopped	**1**
125 g	okra, finely sliced	**4 oz**
2	small ripe mangoes	**2**
12	spring onions, finely sliced	**12**
6 tbsp	chopped parsley	**6 tbsp**

½	fresh lime, cut into slices, for garnish	**½**
	Coriander Sauce	
20 g	fresh coriander leaves	**¾ oz**
4	spring onions, roughly chopped	**4**
1	garlic clove, roughly chopped	**1**
½	onion, roughly chopped	**½**
1 cm	piece fresh ginger root, peeled and roughly chopped	**½ inch**
½	green chili pepper, seeded and roughly chopped	**½**
	freshly ground black pepper	
4 tsp	wine vinegar	**4 tsp**
½	fresh lime, juice only	**½**
2 tbsp	virgin olive oil	**2 tbsp**

Blend all the sauce ingredients with 2 tbsp water until smooth. Set aside.

Boil the rice in the vegetable stock with the garlic and seasoning, for about 20 mins, until cooked.

Halve the bananas lengthwise, without peeling. Score the skin through to the flesh in a few places. Put in a pan, cover with cold water and add the vinegar. Bring to the boil and simmer for 20 mins. Drain and peel. Cut each lengthwise into 3 or 4 slices. Keep them warm.

Meanwhile, put the carrot in a steamer and steam it for 3 mins; add the red pepper, celery and okra and steam for 5 more mins, until cooked but still crisp. Keep them warm.

Peel the mangoes, cut off the two cheeks from each and slice them. Dice the remaining flesh.

Add the diced mangoes, spring onions, vegetables and parsley to the rice. Serve with bananas, mango slices, a slice of lime and the coriander sauce.

Basmati and Wild Rice Moulds with Artichokes

Serves 6

Working time: about 1 hour and 30 minutes

Total time: about 2 hours and 30 minutes (includes soaking)

Calories 405
Protein 14g
Cholesterol 25mg
Total fat 12g
Saturated fat 5g
Sodium 245mg

125 g	wild rice	**4 oz**
125 g	basmati rice, rinsed under cold running water, then soaked in 60 cl (1 pint) water for 1 hour	**4 oz**
½ tsp	salt	**½ tsp**
6	globe artichokes	**6**
2	lemons, grated rind of 1, juice of both	**2**

1 tbsp	virgin olive oil	**1 tbsp**
3 tbsp	chopped mint	**3 tbsp**
2	garlic cloves, finely chopped	**2**
125 g	fresh chestnuts, peeled, or 60 g (2 oz) dried chestnuts, soaked overnight	**4 oz**
60 g	unsalted butter	**2 oz**
	white pepper	

Bring 1.25 litres (2 pints) of water to the boil. Stir in the wild rice, simmer, uncovered, until *al dente* – about 45 mins. Drain the basmati rice and place in a large pan with the salt, add 90 cl (1½ pints) of water, and boil uncovered, for 5 mins until cooked. Drain, and set it aside.

While the wild rice is cooking, put 3 litres (5 pints) of water in a bowl and add ⅓ of the lemon juice. Cut the stem off the artichokes. Discard the outer leaves, until you reach the pale yellow leaves at the core. Cut the top ⅔ off. Trim away any dark green leaf bases from the bottom. Cut the bottom in ½ and remove the hairy choke and all the pinkish central leaves. Then cut each ½ into 6 wedges. Drop the wedges into the acidulated water.

Heat the oil in a frying pan over medium heat. Add the mint and garlic, cook for about 1 min. Drain the artichokes, add to the pan and stir-fry for 1 min. Add remaining lemon juice and ¼ litre '(8 fl oz) of water, cover and simmer for about 10 mins. Remove the lid, cook for a further 5 to 10 mins, until artichokes are tender.

Drain the wild rice. Chop the chestnuts finely. Melt the butter in a pan, add the chestnuts and fry for 2 to 3 min. Add both rice, mix well and heat through. Divide among 6 moulds or cups and turn out on hot plates.

Arrange the artichoke wedges beside the rice. Add the lemon rind and some white pepper to the juices left in the pan and spoon over artichokes before serving.

Pumpkin and Pecorino Risotto

Serves 4

Working (and total) time: about 1 hour and 15 minutes

Calories 305
Protein 6g
Cholesterol 5mg
Total fat 6g
Saturated fat 2g
Sodium 280mg

1 tbsp	virgin olive oil	1 tbsp
2	shallots, finely chopped	2
250 g	Italian round-grain rice	8 oz
500 g	pumpkin, peeled, seeded and finely grated	1 lb
¼ tsp	powdered saffron	¼ tsp
8 cl	dry white wine	3 fl oz
90 cl	unsalted vegetable stock	1½ pints
1 tbsp	finely chopped fresh oregano, 1 tsp dried oregano	1 tbsp
½ tsp	salt	½ tsp
	freshly ground black pepper	
30 g	pecorino cheese, finely grated	1 oz
2 tbsp	finely chopped flat-leaf parsley, for garnish (optional)	2 tbsp

Heat the oil in a 2 to 3 litre (3½ to 5 pint) casserole. Add the shallots, cook over medium heat for about 5 mins, stirring occasionally, until soft but not brown. Reduce the heat, add the rice, and stir to coat with the oil. Add the pumpkin and stir over medium heat for about 3 mins, until heated through. Stir the saffron into the wine. Increase the heat and pour the wine into the casserole. Stir until the liquid has been absorbed – about 3 mins. Meanwhile, heat the stock in a separate pan.

Reduce the heat under the rice and ladle in about 15 cl (¼ pint) of hot stock. Stir, then place the lid on the casserole to almost cover the top.

Simmer, until all the stock has been absorbed – about 5 minutes. Stir in another ladleful of stock and cover as before. This time, stir once or twice while the stock is being absorbed, replacing lid after stirring. Mix in the oregano, then continue to add stock by the ladleful, stirring, until the rice is soft but still has a bite, and the pumpkin has almost melted into the sauce – about 30 mins. Stir in the remaining stock and replace the lid. Turn off the heat and leave to stand for 5 mins. The remaining stock will be absorbed.

Season the risotto with the salt, some pepper and the cheese, stirring until the cheese has melted. Garnish with parsley. Serve.

Pea and Mushroom Risotto

Serves 6

Working time: about 45 minutes

Total time: about 1 hour and 15 minutes

Calories 410

Protein 12g

Cholesterol 20mg

Total fat 10g

Saturated fat 5g

Sodium 430mg

350 g	.peas, shelled, or 125 g (4 oz) frozen peas thawed	**12 oz**	**250 g**	tomatoes, skinned, seeded, and chopped	**8 oz**
30 g	unsalted butter	**1 oz**	**½ tsp**	salt	**½ tsp**
125 g	shallots, chopped	**4 oz**	**250 g**	chestnut mushrooms, wiped clean and coarsely grated	**8 oz**
500 g	brown round-grain rice	**1 lb**	**60 g**	Parmesan cheese, grated freshly ground black pepper chopped parsley for garnish	**2 oz**
20 cl	dry white wine or dry vermouth	**7 fl oz**			
45 cl	tomato juice	**¾ pint**			
45 cl	unsalted vegetable stock	**¾ pint**			

If using fresh peas, boil until barely tender – 3 to 4 minutes. Drain, then refresh them under cold running water. Drain them again and set aside. (frozen peas do not need precooking.)

In a large saucepan, melt the butter and sauté the shallots over medium heat until they are transparent, stirring occasionally – 3 to 5 minutes. Stir the rice into the shallots and cook it for 2 to 3 minutes, stirring constantly to ensure that the grains are well coated with the butter.

Pour the wine into the rice and simmer, stirring frequently, until the wine has been absorbed by the rice. Pour in the tomato juice and 30 cl (½ pint) of the stock, bring the liquid

to the boil, then reduce the heat to a simmer. Cover the saucepan and cook the rice, stirring occasionally, for about 20 minutes. Stir the tomatoes and salt into the rice, cover and simmer for a further 10 minutes, adding more stock, a ladleful at a time, if the rice dries out.

Add the mushrooms, peas and any remaining stock to the pan, increase the heat to high and cook rapidly, stirring constantly, until the stock is absorbed but the rice is still very moist. Stir the pasmesan cheese into the risotto and season it generously with freshly ground pepper. Turn the risotto into a warmed serving dish and sprinkle it with chopped parsley.

Rice Cakes with Onion Relish

Serves 4

Working time: about 35 minutes

Total time: about 1 hour and 45 minutes (includes soaking)

Calories 255

Protein 8g

Cholesterol 15mg

Total fat 6g

Saturated fat 3g

Sodium 300mg

175 g	basmati rice, rinsed under cold running water until the water runs clear, then soaked for 1 hour in 1 litre (1¾ pints) water	**6 oz**
¼ tsp	safflower oil	**¼ tsp**
1	onion, finely chopped	**1**
125 g	carrots, grated	**4 oz**
2	hot green chili peppers, finely chopped	**2**
2	garlic cloves, crushed	**2**
½ tsp	cardamom seeds, crushed	**½ tsp**
1 tbsp	chopped fresh coriander	**1 tbsp**
½ tsp	ground cumin	**½ tsp**
¼ tsp	ground turmeric	**¼ tsp**
60 g	Cheddar cheese, grated	**2 oz**
¼ tsp	salt	**¼ tsp**

Onion Relish

1	onion, cut into paper-thin rings	**1**
½	sweet red pepper, finely chopped	**½**
1	lime, finely grated rind and juice	**1**
¼ tsp	salt	**¼ tsp**
½ tsp	paprika	**½ tsp**
½ tsp	brown sugar	**½ tsp**

First make the relish. Place the onion in a bowl with the red pepper, and add the lime rind and juice, salt, paprika and sugar. Toss the ingredients until well combined, then transfer them to a serving bowl and set them aside.

Drain the rice and put it in a large pan, add 1.5 litres (2½ pints) of water and boil. Boil rapidly, uncovered, until tender – about 10 mins. Drain, and set it aside.

Heat the oil in a frying pan over medium heat and fry the onion, until softened and beginning to brown. Stir in the carrots, chili peppers, garlic, cardamom, coriander, cumin and turmeric, cook, stirring, until the carrots have softened – about 2 mins. Remove from the heat, stir in the rice, cheese and salt, mash with a potato masher, until rice is broken up and sticky.

Preheat the grill to medium. Flour your hands and shape the mixture into 20 balls. Thread onto 4 skewers. Place on a foil-covered rack and grill for about 15 minutes, turning once, until they are a pale golden. Serve hot, with the onion relish.

Semolina Gnocchi with Julienned Vegetables

Serves 6

Working time: about 1 hour

Total time: about 3 hours (includes chilling)

Calories 270

Protein 13g

Cholesterol 5mg

Total fat 8g

Saturated fat 3g

Sodium 295mg

250 g	celeriac, finely julienned, placed in acidulted water	**8 oz**
350 g	carrots, finely julienned	**12 oz**
18	spring onions, trimmed, quartered lengthwise and cut into 5 cm (2 inch) pieces	**18**
3	garlic cloves, crushed	**3**
30 cl	unsalted vegetable stock	**½ pint**
½	lemon, grated rind and juice	**½**
1½ tsp	cornflour	**1½ tsp**
30 g	pine-nuts	**1 oz**

½ tsp	caster sugar	**½ tsp**
½ tsp	salt	**½ tsp**
	freshly ground black pepper	
	Semolina Gnocchi	
60 cl	skimmed milk	**1 pint**
200 g	semolina	**7 oz**
15 g	unsalted butter	**½ oz**
½ tsp	salt	**½ tsp**
½ tsp	freshly grated nutmeg	**½ tsp**
4 tbsp	freshly grated Parmesan cheese	**4 tbsp**

Bring the milk to the boil, add the semolina gradually, stirring constantly, then cook for 4-5 mins over medium heat until very thick. Beat in half the butter, the salt, the nutmeg and 3 tbsp of the cheese. Spread out in an 18 by 18 by 4 cm (7 by 7 by 1½ inch) tray lined with plastic film. Cool for 20 mins, cover loosely and chill in the refrigerator for 2 hrs.

Preheat the oven to 180°C (350°F or Mark 4). Cut the mixture into 36 2.5 cm (1 inch) squares. Transfer to a lightly greased baking sheet. Melt the remaining butter and brush it over the gnocchi. Sprinkle with the remaining cheese. Bake until golden crisp on top – 20 to 25 mins.

15 mins before the gnocchi are cooked, put the vegetables and garlic into a pan with the stock. Boil, then simmer for 2 to 4 mins, until vegetables are soft. Stir in the lemon rind and juice, and the cornflour, blended with 1 tbsp of water. Add the pine-nuts, sugar, salt and pepper. Boil, stirring, until a thick sauce has formed.

Serve the vegetables on warm plates, topped with baked gnocchi.

Chili Beans with Cornbread Topping

Serves 4

Working time: about 30 minutes

Total time: about 3 hours (includes soaking)

Calories 340

Protein 15g

Cholesterol 60mg

Total fat 10g

Saturated fat 1g

Sodium 405mg

100 g	red kidney beans, picked over	**3½ oz**
1 tbsp	safflower oil	**1 tbsp**
1	onion, chopped	**1**
½ tsp	chili powder	**½ tsp**
2	garlic cloves, chopped	**2**
750 g	ripe tomatoes, skinned, seeded, chopped, or 400 g/14 oz can	**1½ lb**
1	sweet red and green pepper, seeded, deribbed and coarsely chopped	**1**
2	sticks celery, trimmed and sliced	**2**
1 tbsp	tomato paste	**1 tbsp**

60 g	green olives, quartered or halved	**2 oz**
	Cornbread Topping	
125 g	cornmeal	**4 oz**
30 g	strong plain flour	**1 oz**
¼ tsp	salt	**¼ tsp**
¼ tsp	freshly ground black pepper	**¼ tsp**
2 tsp	baking powder	**2 tsp**
1	egg, beaten	**1**
12.5 cl	skimmed milk	**4 fl oz**
2 tbsp	chopped parsley	**2 tbsp**
30 g	Edam cheese, finely grated	**1 oz**

Rinse the beans, put in a pan with cold water covering them by about 7.5 cm (3 ins). Discard beans that float to the surface. Boil, with lid ajar, for 2 mins. Leave to soak and cool for 1 hr.

Rinse the beans, place in a clean pan, cover with water. Boil for 10 mins, rinse. Cover again with fresh water, simmer until tender – about 1 hour.

Preheat the oven to 200°C (400°F or Mark 6).

Heat the oil in a pan, and fry the onion until soft. Add the chili and garlic and fry for 1 min. Stir in the tomatoes, peppers, celery and tomato paste, cover, cook over medium-low heat for 10 mins. Add the olives and beans, cook for 5 mins more, stirring occasionally. Divide mixture among 4 shallow dishes and set aside.

Mix the dry topping ingredients and make a well in the centre. In a separate bowl, beat together the egg, milk and parsley, pour into the cornflour and beat until the mixture is smooth and thick. Spread over the chili beans, sprinkle with cheese and bake until topping is firm – 15 to 20 mins.

Polenta Pizza

Serves 4

Working
time: about
40 minutes

Total time:
about
1 hour

Calories
470
Protein
19g
Cholesterol
25mg
Total fat
12g
Saturated fat
5g
Sodium
390mg

½ tsp	salt	½ tsp
350 g	cornmeal	12 oz
1 tbsp	virgin olive oil	1 tbsp
1	red onion, finely sliced	1
1	large garlic clove, chopped	1
2	carrots, chopped	2
4	sticks celery, finely sliced	4
500 g	tomatoes, skinned, seeded and chopped	1 lb
6 tbsp	tomato paste, dissolved in 17.5 cl (6 fl oz) hot water	6 tbsp
1 tbsp	chopped fresh basil, or 1 tsp dried basil	1 tbsp
½ tbsp	chopped fresh oregano, or ½ tsp dried oregano	½ tbsp
	cayenne pepper	
	freshly ground black pepper	
125 g	low-fat mozzarella cheese, very thinly sliced	4 oz
1 tbsp	freshly grated Parmesan cheese	1 tbsp
½ tbsp	finely chopped parsley, for garnish	½ tbsp

Preheat the oven to 180°C (350°F or Mark 4). Thoroughly grease a 30 by 22 by 2.5 cm (12 by 9 by 1 inch) baking tin or dish.

Put 1.6 litres (2¾ pints) of water into a pan with the salt, and bring it to the boil. Sprinkle in the cornmeal, stirring continuously. Reduce the heat to medium and cook, stirring constantly, until the polenta is quite stiff – 10 to 15 mins. Spoon into the baking tin and spread it out evenly. Cover with foil, and bake for 20 mins.

Meanwhile, make the sauce. Heat the oil in a pan, add the onion and sauté until soft and transparent – about 10 mins. Add the garlic, carrots, celery and tomatoes. Stir well for a few minutes, then add the tomato paste solution. Finally, add the basil, oregano, some cayenne and pepper. Simmer, covered, for 10 to 15 mins.

When the polenta is ready, spread the sauce over it. Cover with the mozzarella, then sprinkle over the Parmesan. Return to the oven for about 10 mins, until the cheese has melted. Serve immediately, garnished with parsley.

Polenta Ring with Pine-Nuts and Mozzarella

Serves 6

Working time: about 45 minutes

Total time: about 1 hour and 45 minutes (includes cooling)

Calories 300
Protein 13g
Cholesterol 20mg
Total fat 14g
Saturated fat 4g
Sodium 265mg

500 g	tomatoes, skinned	1 lb
2 tbsp	virgin olive oil	2 tbsp
1 tsp	paprika	1 tsp
2	garlic cloves, one crushed the other chopped	2
½ tsp	salt	½ tsp
150 g	cornmeal	5 oz
125 g	low-fat mozzarella cheese, thinly sliced	4 oz
1	onion, thinly sliced	1
1	sweet red pepper, seeded, deribbed and cut into 2.5 cm (1 inch) strips	1
1	sweet green pepper, seeded, deribbed and cut into 2.5 cm (1 inch) strips	1
1 tsp	ground cumin	1 tsp
60 g	pine-nuts	2 oz

Thinly slice 3 tomatoes crosswise, and remainder lengthwise; keep them separate. Grease a 20 cm (8 inch) ring mould with ½ tbsp of the oil.

Bring 3 litre (1¼ pints) of water to the boil. Add the paprika, crushed garlic and salt, then stir in the cornmeal. Reduce the heat to medium, cook, stirring, for 10 to 15 mins, until thickened. Remove from the heat and pour half into the mould. Press down firmly. Place the crosswise-sliced tomatoes and the mozzarella on top, and cover with the remaining polenta. Set aside, until completely cool – at least 1 hour.

Preheat the oven to 180°C (350°F or Mark 4). When the polenta has cooled, loosen all around

the edges of the mould. Turn out onto a large, flat plate and bake for about 15 minutes, or until the mozzarella has melted.

Meanwhile, heat the remaining oil in a frying pan over low heat. Put the onion and the chopped garlic in the pan and cook them gently for about 3 mins. Add the peppers, cover, cook over very low heat for 10 mins, add the remaining tomato, cumin and half of the pine-nuts. Cover again and cook gently for 2 mins.

Spoon some of the vegetables into the centre of the polenta ring and remainder round the edge. Sprinkle the remaining pine-nuts over the vegetables. Serve the polenta hot.

Tandoori Patties

Serves 4

Working time: about 45 minutes

Total time: about 2 hours and 45 minutes (includes soaking)

Calories 305
Protein 14g
Cholesterol 0mg
Total fat 6g
Saturated fat 1g
Sodium 290mg

250 g	dried pinto beans, picked over	**8 oz**
1 tbsp	safflower oil	**1 tbsp**
1	onion, chopped	**1**
2	garlic cloves, chopped	**2**
3 tsp	tandoori spice	**3 tsp**
1 tsp	ground cumin	**1 tsp**
30 g	fresh wholemeal breadcrumbs	**1 oz**
2 tbsp	chopped fresh coriander	**2 tbsp**
2 tbsp	tomato paste	**2 tbsp**
125 g	parsnips or carrots, finely grated	**4 oz**
½ tsp	salt	**½ tsp**
	freshly ground black pepper	
3 tbsp	wholemeal flour	**3 tbsp**
1 tsp	paprika	**1 tsp**
	Coriander-Yogurt Sauce	
15 cl	plain low-fat yogurt	**¼ pint**
½ tsp	ground coriander	**½ tsp**
1 tsp	tomato paste	**1 tsp**
1	garlic clove, crushed	**1**
2 tsp	chopped fresh coriander	**2 tsp**

Rinse the beans, put in a pan, with water covering them by about 7.5 cm (3 inches). Discard beans that float to the surface. Cover, the lid ajar, bring to the boil. Boil for 2 mins, turn off heat and soak, covered, for at least 1 hour.

Rinse, return to pan, and cover with water. Bring to the boil. Boil for 10 mins, drain and rinse again. Replace beans and again cover with water. Bring to boil, then simmer until tender – about 1 hour. Add more water if necessary. Drain, rinse, and set them aside.

Heat 2 tbsp of the oil in a frying pan and fry the onion over medium heat for about 3 mins.

Add the garlic, 2 tsps of the tandoori spice, the cumin, and fry for 1 min.

Put the onion mixture and the beans in a food processor or blender with the breadcrumbs, fresh coriander, tomato paste, parsnips or carrots, salt and some pepper. Blend until smooth.

Preheat the grill to medium high. Mix the flour with remaining tandoori spice and the paprika. Shape into 8 patties. Coat with flour. Brush with the oil and grill for 3 to 4 mins on each side, until they are crisp.

Mix all the sauce ingredients together. Serve the patties hot, with the coriander-yogurt sauce.

Butter Beans Baked with a Herbed Crust

Serves 6

Working time: about 30 minutes

Total time: about 3 hours (includes soaking)

Calories 310

Protein 19g

Cholesterol 0mg

Total fat 5g

Saturated fat 1g

Sodium 280mg

500 g	dried butter beans, picked over	**1 lb**
2	onions, one finely chopped	**2**
1	large carrot, trimmed	**1**
1	small leek, trimmed, washed	**1**
2	fresh thyme sprigs, one chopped	**2**
2	fresh rosemary sprigs, one chopped	**2**
2	bay leaves	**2**
1½ tbsp	virgin olive oil	**1½ tbsp**

1.5 kg	fresh tomatoes, skinned, seeded and roughly chopped	**3 lb**
2	garlic cloves, one crushed, one chopped	**2**
1 tsp	salt	**1 tsp**
	freshly ground black pepper	
125 g	fresh wholemeal breadcrumbs	**4 oz**
30 g	parsley, chopped	**1 oz**
1	lemon, grated rind only	**1**

Rinse the beans, put in a pan with water to cover them by about 7.5 cm (3 ins). Discard any that float to the surface. Cover, lid ajar, and bring to the boil. Boil for 2 mins, then soak, covered, for at least 1 hr.

Rinse, place in a pan, covered with water as before. Bring to the boil. Boil for 10 mins, drain and rinse again. Put in a pan with the whole vegetables, herb sprigs and 1 bay leaf. Cover well with water and bring to the boil. Simmer, covered, until tender – about 1 hr. Add more water if necessary. Drain the beans and discard the vegetables and herbs.

Heat 1 tsp of the oil in a pan, add the chopped onion, half the chopped herbs, remaining bay leaf, and sauté for 3 mins. Add tomatoes and crushed garlic, bring to boil. Season, then simmer, uncovered, for 30 to 40 mins, until reduced to a sauce.

Preheat the oven to 180°C (350°F or Mark 4). Mix the chopped garlic, remaining rosemary and thyme, breadcrumbs and parsley. Add the lemon rind and remaining oil, and mix well.

When the tomato mixture is ready, stir in the beans, transfer to a large gratin dish. Spread the herbed crumbs on top and bake uncovered for 40 mins, until the crust is crisp.

Butter Bean Succotash

Serves 4

Working time: about 30 minutes

Total time: about 2 hours and 45 minutes (includes soaking)

Calories 325
Protein 15g
Cholesterol 10mg
Total fat 6g
Saturated fat 2g
Sodium 300mg

200 g	dried butter beans, picked over	7 oz	1	savory sprig	1
½ tbsp	safflower oil	½ tbsp	350 g	fresh or frozen sweetcorn kernels	12 oz
1	onion, sliced	1	½ tsp	salt	½ tsp
2	garlic cloves, crushed	2	1 tsp	sugar	1 tsp
3	sticks celery, trimmed and sliced	3		freshly ground black pepper	
1	large potato, chopped	1	3 tbsp	soured cream	3 tbsp
1	sweet green pepper, seeded, deribbed and chopped	1	1 tsp	fresh lemon juice	1 tsp
			2 tbsp	chopped parsley	2 tbsp

Rinse the beans, put into a large pan with water to cover them by about 7.5 cm (3 inches). Discard any that float to the surface. Cover, lid ajar, and bring to the boil. Boil for 2 minutes, then turn off the heat and soak, covered, for at least 1 hr.

Rinse, place in pan and cover with water as before. Bring to the boil. Boil for 10 mins, then drain and rinse again.

Put into a pan, and cover with water again. Bring to boil, reduce the heat, simmer, cook until tender – about 1 hour. Add more water if necessary. Drain, over a bowl, and reserve the liquid. Rinse the beans under cold water. Drain them again, and set aside.

Heat the oil in a pan and fry the onion for about 3 minutes, until soft. Add the garlic, celery, potato, green pepper, savory and the reserved bean-cooking liquid, made up to 60 cl (1 pint) with water, if necessary. Cover the pan, bring to the boil and simmer for 10 minutes.

Add the cooked beans to the saucepan, with the sweetcorn, salt, sugar and some black pepper. Cook the mixture for a further 10 minutes. Remove the pan from the heat and stir in the soured cream and lemon juice. Ladle the succotash into individual bowls and sprinkle over the chopped parsley.

Cabbage with Black-Eyed Peas and Mushrooms

Serves 4

Working time: about 1 hour

Total time: about 3 hours and 15 minutes

Calories 155
Protein 8g
Cholesterol 20mg
Total fat 7g
Saturated fat 2g
Sodium 220mg

60 g	dried black-eyed peas, picked over	**2 oz**
1 tbsp	virgin olive oil	**1 tbsp**
15 g	unsalted butter	**½ oz**
1	firm green cabbage (1 kg/2½ lb), hollowed out, 250 g (8 oz) inner leaves reserved and chopped	**1**
3	garlic cloves, chopped	**3**
1	onion, chopped	**1**
125 g	mushrooms, wiped clean and chopped	**4 oz**
15 g	flaked millet	**½ oz**
15 cl	unsalted vegetable stock	**¼ pint**
½ tsp	salt	**½ tsp**
	freshly ground black pepper	
1 tbsp	finely chopped fresh coriander	**1 tbsp**
1 tbsp	finely chopped summer savory	**1 tbsp**

Rinse the peas, put into a pan with water to cover them by about 7.5 cm (3 ins). Discard any that float to the surface. Bring to the boil, cook for 2 mins. Cover, and soak for at least 1 hr.

Rinse the peas. Place in a pan and cover with water as before. Bring to the boil, cover tightly and simmer, skimming any foam from the surface, until tender – about 1 hr. Add hot water if necessary. Drain, rinse and set aside.

Preheat the oven to 200°C (400°F or Mark 6).

In a frying pan, heat the oil and butter. Add the chopped cabbage, garlic, onion and mushrooms, cook, stirring, for 5 to 7 mins, until softened but not browned. Remove from the heat. Stir in the cooked peas. Add the millet and the stock. Stir, and bring to a simmer. Simmer for 5 mins. Remove from the heat, season and add the herbs.

Fill the hollowed-out cabbage with the stuffing. Put the cabbage 'lid' on, and enclose the whole in parchment paper.

Place on a baking sheet and bake for 30 to 40 mins. Leave to rest for a few mins before unwrapping and serving.

Chick-Pea and Okra Casserole with Couscous

Serves 4	
Working time: about 30 minutes	
Total time: about 3 hours and 30 minutes (includes soaking)	

Calories 450	
Protein 15g	
Cholesterol 0mg	
Total fat 10g	
Saturated fat 1g	
Sodium 320mg	

125 g	dried chick-peas, picked over	4 oz	½ tsp	salt	½ tsp
2 tbsp	virgin olive oil	2 tbsp	250 g	carrots, thickly sliced	8 oz
1	large onion, chopped	1	60 g	dried apricots	2 oz
1 tbsp	paprika	1 tbsp	125 g	baby sweetcorn	4 oz
1 tsp	ground turmeric	1 tsp	125 g	dried pears	4 oz
3	fresh thyme sprigs	3	30 g	currants	1 oz
2	fresh bay leaves	2	250 g	small okra, trimmed	8 oz
90 cl	unsalted vegetable stock or water	1½ pints	250 g	wholemeal couscous	8 oz

Rinse the chick-peas, put in a pan with water to cover them by about 7.5cm (3 inches). Discard any that float to the surface. Cover, lid ajar, and bring to the boil. Boil for 2 mins, cool and soak for at least 1 hr.

Drain, rinse, and return to the pan, cover with water as before. Bring to the boil, reduce the heat, simmer until just tender – about 1 hour. If the peas appear to be drying out add more hot water. Drain, and rinse.

In a large pan, heat half the oil and sauté the onion over medium heat until transparent – about 3 mins. Add paprika and turmeric, cook, stirring for 1 to 2 mins. Add the thyme, bay

leaves, chick-peas and stock and bring to the boil. Reduce the heat, cover and simmer for 45 mins. Add salt, carrots, apricots, sweetcorn, pears and currants. Cover, simmer for 15 mins.

Heat the remaining oil and sauté the okra for 5 mins. Add to the vegetables and simmer for 15 mins.

Place the couscous in a bowl and pour ½ litre (16 fl oz) of boiling water over it. Stir with a fork, then leave it to absorb the water – about 10 mins. Arrange the couscous on a serving dish and pile the fruit and vegetable stew in the centre, discarding the bay leaves and thyme sprigs.

Chick-Pea and Burghul Kofta

Serves 4

Working
time: about
45 minutes

Total time:
about
4 hours
(includes
soaking and
chilling)

Calories
430
Protein
21g
Cholesterol
0mg
Total fat
12g
Saturated fat
2g
Sodium
60mg

250 g	dried chick-peas, picked over	**8 oz**
125 g	burghul, soaked in warm water for 30 minutes, drained and squeezed dry in paper towels	**4 oz**
2 tbsp	tahini	**2 tbsp**
6 tbsp	plain low-fat yogurt	**6 tbsp**
1	lemon, juice only lettuce leaves, washed and dried, and lemon wedges, for garnish	**1**
	Chili-Tomato Relish	
1 tbsp	virgin olive oil	**1 tbsp**
500 g	tomatoes, chopped	**1 lb**
1	small onion, very finely chopped	**1**
1	cucumber, very finely chopped	**1**
2–3	fresh hot red or green chili peppers, seeded and finely chopped	**2–3**

Rinse the chick-peas under cold running water, then transfer them to a large pan and pour in enough water to cover them by about 7.5 cm (3 inches). Discard any that float to the surface. Cover the pan, leaving the lid ajar, and bring to the boil. Boil for 2 minutes, then turn off the heat, cover, and soak for at least 1 hour.

Drain and rinse the chick-peas, return them to the pan covered with water as before. Bring to the boil, reduce the heat to maintain a simmer and cook the peas, covered, until they are soft – about 1½ hours – adding more hot water as required.

Drain the chick-peas, then purée them in a food processor. Stir in the burghul, tahini, yogurt,

onion, garlic, parsley, mint and lemon juice. Using your hands, form the mixture into 16 boat shapes; chill them for 1 hour.

Meanwhile, begin to make the relish. Heat the oil in a heavy-bottomed pan over low heat. Add the tomatoes and cook them gently, covered, for 15 minutes. Sieve the tomatoes and chill the purée for 1 hour.

Preheat the grill to high and cover a grill rack with foil. Grill the kofta until golden-brown – 3 to 4 minutes on each side. Meanwhile, stir the onion, cucumber and chilies into the tomato purée. Serve the kofta hot, garnished with the lettuce leaves and lemon wedges.

Indonesian Vegetable Stew

200 g	small aubergines, cut into 1 cm (½ inch) cubes	**7 oz**
1 tsp	salt	**1 tsp**
3 tbsp	safflower oil	**3 tbsp**
1 tbsp	black mustard seeds	**1 tbsp**
1 tbsp	ground fenugreek	**1 tbsp**
2	dried hot red chili peppers, seeded, and broken into small pieces	**2**
2	fresh hot green chili peppers, seeded, and thinly sliced	**2**
6	garlic cloves, chopped	**6**
1 tsp	freshly ground green cardamom pods	**1 tsp**
1 tsp	concentrated tamarind paste	**1 tsp**
125 g	dried mung beans, picked over, rinsed	**4 oz**
1.25 l	unsalted vegetable stock	**2 pints**
500 g	potatoes, thickly sliced	**1 lb**
125 g	dried ceps, soaked in hot water for 20 minutes, drained and roughly chopped	**4 oz**
250 g	okra, trimmed and sliced	**8 oz**
500 g	French beans, trimmed and halved	**1 lb**
2	spears fresh lemon grass, finely chopped	**2**
1	lemon, grated rind and juice	**1**
2 tbsp	grated creamed coconut	**2 tbsp**

Toss the aubergines with the salt. Place in a colander, weight them down with a plate and let them drain for 30 mins. Rinse and drain.

Meanwhile, in a large saucepan, heat the oil over medium-high heat. Add the mustard seeds, fenugreek, dried and fresh chili peppers, garlic, cardamom and tamarind paste. Sauté these for about 2 mins, stirring occasionally, add the mung beans and stock. Bring to the boil, reduce the heat and simmer, uncovered, for 15 minutes.

Add the potatoes, aubergines, ceps and okra to the pan, and simmer, covered, for a further 10 mins. Stir in the French beans, and the lemon grass. Simmer for 10 mins more. Finally, mix in the lemon rind, lemon juice and coconut and simmer for 1 min more. Before serving, allow the stew to rest, uncovered, for about 5 minutes, to allow the flavours to develop.

47

Lentils with Spinach and Carrots

Serves 4

Working time: about 20 minutes

Total time: about 50 minutes

Calories
330

Protein
18g

Cholesterol
0mg

Total fat
10g

Saturated fat
1g

Sodium
80mg

250 g	lentils, picked over and rinsed	**8 oz**
1	bay leaf	**1**
2 tbsp	safflower oil	**2 tbsp**
1	garlic clove, crushed	**1**
1 tbsp	freshly grated ginger root	**1 tbsp**
250 g	carrots, peeled and cut into bâtonnets	**8 oz**
12	spring onions, cut into 2.5 cm (1 inch) lengths	**12**
350 g	spinach, stems discarded, leaves washed, dried and roughly chopped	**12 oz**
2 tbsp	low-sodium soy sauce or shoyu	**2 tbsp**
6 tbsp	dry sherry	**6 tbsp**
1 tbsp	sesame seeds, toasted	**1 tbsp**

Put the lentils in a large, heavy-bottomed saucepan with ¾ litre (1¼ pints) of water. Bring to the boil, then reduce the heat to medium, add the bay leaf, cover the pan tightly and simmer the lentils until tender – about 40 minutes. Drain the lentils and remove the bay leaf. Rinse and drain lentils again.

Heat the oil in a wok or large, heavy frying pan over high heat. Add the garlic and ginger, and stir until the garlic sizzles. Add the carrots and spring onions and stir-fry for 1 min, then transfer to a plate using a slotted spoon.

Place the spinach in the pan and stir it over high heat until it begins to wilt – 2 to 3 minutes. Return the carrots and spring onions to the pan,

add the cooked lentils and stir them for 2 minutes to heat them through. Add the soy sauce and the sherry and bring them to the boil. Stir the ingredients once more, then transfer them to a heated serving dish. Scatter the toasted sesame seeds over the lentils and vegetables, and serve immediately.

Suggested accompaniment: long-grain brown rice.

Editor's Note: To toast the sesame seeds, heat them in a small, heavy frying pan over medium-low heat until they are golden – 1 to 2 minutes.

Lentil and Potato Cakes with Mustard Pickle

Serves 4

Working time: about 40 minutes

Total time: about 1 hour and 40 minutes

Calories 295
Protein 15g
Cholesterol 10mg
Total fat 4g
Saturated fat 1g
Sodium 245mg

250 g	floury potatoes, peeled and cut into 2.5 cm (1 inch) cubes	**8 oz**
½ tsp	safflower oil	**½ tsp**
12	spring onions, trimmed, white parts chopped, green parts sliced into rings	**12**
2.5 cm	ginger root, peeled and chopped	**1 inch**
¼ tsp	ground cinnamon	**¼ tsp**
¼ tsp	grated nutmeg	**¼ tsp**
½ tsp	salt	**½ tsp**
	freshly ground black pepper	
175 g	split red lentils, picked over, rinsed	**6 oz**
45 cl	unsalted vegetable stock	**¾ pint**
½ tsp	garam masala	**½ tsp**
175 g	thick Greek yogurt	**6 oz**
	Mustard Pickle	
¼ tsp	safflower oil	**¼ tsp**
1	small onion, finely chopped	**1**
1 tbsp	mustard seeds, lightly crushed	**1 tbsp**
2 tbsp	white wine vinegar	**2 tbsp**
4 tbsp	dry white wine	**4 tbsp**
1 tbsp	soft brown sugar	**1 tbsp**
1 tbsp	grainy mustard	**1 tbsp**
1	red-skinned mango, peeled and stoned, flesh roughly diced	**1**

First make the pickle. Heat the oil, add the onion and mustard seeds, stir over medium heat for about 3 mins, until the onions are soft. Stir in the other ingredients. Bring to the boil, then cover and cook gently for about 15 mins, until tender, thick and pulpy. Transfer to a bowl.

Boil, drain and mash the potatoes.

Heat the oil in a frying pan and add the white spring onion, ginger, cinnamon, nutmeg, seasoning. Stir over medium heat for 3 mins. Add the lentils and stock. Bring to the boil, then

cover and simmer for about 25 mins, stirring frequently, until lentils are soft. Remove the lid and increase the heat, stirring until the mixture is dry – about 2 mins. Beat in the potatoes and garam masala; cool.

Preheat the grill to medium. Shape the mixture into 12 flat cakes and place them on a greased baking sheet. Grill for 5 mins on each side, until golden. Serve topped with yogurt and pickle, garnished with green spring onion rings.

Lentils with Cumin and Onion

Serves 4		
Working time: about 15 minutes		
Total time: about 1 hour		

Calories 215		
Protein 9g		
Cholesterol 0mg		
Total fat 7g		
Saturated fat 1g		
Sodium 225mg		

350 g	lentils, picked over and rinsed	**12 oz**
1 tsp	ground cumin	**1 tsp**
½ tsp	salt	**½ tsp**
60 g	brown rice	**2 oz**

1 tbsp	virgin olive oil	**1 tbsp**
500 g	onions, thinly sliced	**1 lb**
90 g	radishes, thinly sliced	**3 oz**
2 tbsp	chopped parsley	**2 tbsp**

In a heavy-bottomed saucepan, bring 1.5 litres (2½ pints) of water to the boil. Add the lentils, cumin and salt, and boil, uncovered, for 20 minutes. Add the rice and cook for a further 30 to 40 minutes, until the liquid has been absorbed but the rice is still moist.

Meanwhile, heat the oil in a frying pan, and fry the onions over low heat, partially covered, until they are soft and golden-brown, stirring them frequently while they are cooking – about 15 minutes.

Stir half of the fried onions into the lentils. Transfer the mixture to the centre of a shallow serving dish. Distribute the remaining fried onions round the lentil mixture, then arrange the radishes round the onions at the edge of the dish. Sprinkle the chopped parsley over the lentils. serve hot.

Suggested accompaniment: salad of lettuce and cucumber.

Lentil Soufflés Baked in Sweet Pepper Cases

Serves 6

Working time: about 40 minutes

Total time: about 2 hours

Calories 165
Protein 10g
Cholesterol 75mg
Total fat 5g
Saturated fat 1g
Sodium 130mg

1 tbsp	virgin olive oil	1 tbsp
1	large onion, finely chopped	1
1	large carrot, finely chopped	1
1	garlic clove, crushed	1
175 g	split red lentils, picked over, rinsed	6 oz
45 cl	unsalted vegetable stock	¾ pint
¼ tsp	salt	¼ tsp
2 tbsp	tomato paste	2 tbsp
3	large sweet green peppers	3
	freshly ground black pepper	
2	eggs, separated	2

Heat the oil in a large, heavy-bottomed saucepan over medium heat. Add the onion and carrot and cook gently for 5 minutes. Stir in the garlic, lentils, stock, salt and tomato paste. Bring the mixture to the boil, then reduce the heat, cover the pan tightly and simmer for 45 minutes, until the lentils are soft and the stock has been absorbed.

Meanwhile, carefully remove the stalk from each pepper. Cut the peppers in half horizontally and remove their seeds and any thick white ribs. Cook the pepper cups in gently simmering water to cover for 4 to 5 minutes until softened, then drain them well on paper towels. Place the cups in a lightly oiled, shallow ovenproof dish.

Preheat the oven to 190°C (375°F or Mark 5).

Remove the cooked lentils from the heat and allow them to cool for 10 minutes. Season with some pepper, then beat in the egg yolks. Whisk the egg whites until stiff but not dry; fold 1 tablespoon into the lentil mixture to lighten it, then fold in the remainder. Spoon the soufflé mixture into the pepper cups and cook for 30 to 35 minutes, until the soufflés are well risen and lightly browned. Serve immediately.

Suggested accompaniments: tomato salad; crusty bread.

Tofu with Sweet Pepper and Peanuts, Sichuan Style

Serves 6

Working (and total) time: about 35 minutes

Calories
220
Protein
15g
Cholesterol
0mg
Total fat
15g
Saturated fat
1g
Sodium
50mg

2 tbsp	safflower oil	**2 tbsp**
1 kg	firm tofu, well drained, cut into 2 cm (¾ inch) cubes	**2 lb**
2	garlic cloves, thinly sliced	**2**
4 cm	piece fresh ginger root, peeled and finely shredded	**1½ inch**
3	fresh or dried red chili peppers, seeded and thinly sliced	**3**
8	spring onions, green and white parts separated and thinly sliced	**8**
2	small sweet green peppers, seeded, deribbed, cut into small squares	**2**

⅛ tsp	salt	**⅛ tsp**
1 tbsp	rice wine or sherry	**1 tbsp**
45 g	shelled peanuts, skinned and toasted	**1½ oz**
	Seasoning Sauce	
2 tbsp	low-sodium soy sauce or shoyu	**2 tbsp**
2 tsp	rice or wine vinegar	**2 tsp**
1½ tsp	sugar	**1½ tsp**
10 cl	vegetable stock or water	**3½ fl oz**
1½ tsp	cornflour	**1½ tsp**
⅛ tsp	Tabasco or chili sauce	**⅛ tsp**

In a frying pan, heat 2 tsps of the oil and fry ½ of the tofu over medium-high for 3 to 5 mins, until golden-brown; turn to prevent the tofu from sticking. Transfer cubes to paper towels to drain. Pour another 2 tsps of the oil into the pan, fry the remaining tofu cubes in the same way.

In a small bowl, mix together all the ingredients for the sauce. Set the sauce aside.

Heat remaining oil in a wok or frying pan. Drop in the garlic, then add the ginger and fry, stirring, until golden-brown – about 2 mins. Add the chilis and white parts of spring onions, and stir-fry for 10 secs, tossing the ingredients. Add sweet peppers, stir-fry for 10 secs, add tofu and stir-fry for a further 20 secs. Add salt and wine.

Stir the sauce well and pour it into the wok. Continue to stir over the heat until the sauce thickens; add the peanuts. Remove the wok from the heat and mix in most of the green parts of the spring onions. Transfer the tofu stir-fry to a serving dish and sprinkle over the remaining spring onions.

Ricotta, Courgette Tortellini with Mint-Yogurt Sauce

Serves 6

Working
(and total)
time: about
1 hour and
40 minutes

Calories
215

Protein
11g

Cholesterol
45mg

Total fat
7g

Saturated fat
4g

Sodium
145mg

175 g	courgettes	6 oz
¼ tsp	salt	¼ tsp
175 g	strong plain flour	6 oz
1	egg	1
1	egg white	1
1 tbsp	safflower oil	1 tbsp
150 g	low-fat ricotta cheese	5 oz
	freshly ground black pepper	

chopped mint leaves, for garnish

Mint-Yogurt Sauce

200 g	low-fat fromage frais	7 oz
100 g	thick Greek yogurt	3½ oz
12.5 cl	plain low-fat yogurt	4 fl oz
4	mint sprigs, leaves only, chopped	4
	white pepper	

Grate the courgettes into a bowl, sprinkle them with the salt and set them aside for 30 minutes.

Make the pasta dough. Put the flour into a bowl, add the egg, egg white and oil, and stir, gradually mixing in the flour. Transfer to a floured surface. Knead until dough comes cleanly away from the surface. Continue kneading until dough is smooth and elastic – about 10 mins. Wrap the dough in plastic film and let it rest for 15 mins.

For the filling; break up the ricotta with a fork and season with black pepper. Squeeze the courgettes dry in muslin and mix with the ricotta.

Divide the dough into 3 equal portions. Cover

2 with plastic film. Roll out the ⅓ on a floured surface into a sheet about 1 mm (¹/₁₆ inch) thick. With a 6 cm (2½ inch) round cutter, cut out 24 circles and form into tortellini, using 1 teaspoon of filling for each. Repeat this with the other 2 pieces of dough.

Blend the sauce ingredients in a processor until smooth. Transfer to a pan and warm gently while you cook the pasta. Do not boil.

Add the tortellini to 3 litres (5 pints) of boiling water with 1½ tsps salt. Start testing 1 min after the water returns to the boil, and cook until they are *al dente*. Drain, and serve immediately with mint-yogurt sauce and chopped mint garnish.

Barley and Mushroom Broth with Smoked Tofu

Serves 4

Working time: about 30 minutes

Total time: about 1 hour

Calories 140
Protein 6g
Cholesterol 0mg
Total fat 5g
Saturated fat trace
Sodium 85mg

60 g	pot barley, rinsed under cold running water and drained	**2 oz**
1.5 litres	unsalted vegetable stock	**2½ pints**
1 tbsp	safflower oil	**1 tbsp**
125 g	onion, finely chopped	**4 oz**
125 g	carrot, diced	**4 oz**
2	sticks celery, diced	**2**
125 g	button mushrooms, wiped clean and sliced	**4 oz**

2 tbsp	mushroom ketchup	**2 tbsp**
2 tbsp	tomato paste	**2 tbsp**
125 g	smoked tofu, cut into 1 cm (½ inch) cubes	**4 oz**
	freshly ground black pepper	
2 tbsp	chopped parsley	**2 tbsp**
2 tbsp	freshly cut chives	**2 tbsp**

Place the barley in a large saucepan with the vegetable stock, and bring the liquid to the boil. Reduce the heat to a simmer, cover the pan and cook the barley for 30 minutes.

Meanwhile, heat the oil in a heavy frying pan, add the onion, carrot and celery, and sweat them over medium heat for about 10 minutes. Add the mushrooms and cook for a further 2 minutes.

Add the sweated vegetables, the mushroom ketchup and the tomato paste to the barley and stock, and simmer, covered, for 20 minutes. Add the tofu to the saucepan and simmer, covered, for a further 10 minutes. Season the broth with some black pepper and stir in the parsley and chives. Serve hot.

Suggested accompaniment: rye bread.

Penne Rigati with Celery and Soft Cheese

Serves 8

**Working
(and total)
time: about
30 minutes**

Calories
320

Protein
14g

Cholesterol
15mg

Total fat
6g

Saturated fat
3g

Sodium
275mg

500 g	penne rigati, or other short, tubular pasta	**1 lb**
250 g	celery, trimmed and finely chopped	**8 oz**
175 g	low-fat soft cheese	**6 oz**
500 g	thick Greek yogurt	**1 lb**
½ tsp	freshly grated nutmeg	**½ tsp**

½ tsp	salt	**½ tsp**
	freshly ground black pepper	
1 tbsp	virgin olive oil	**1 tbsp**
60 g	shallots, finely chopped	**2 oz**
5 tbsp	finely chopped parsley	**5 tbsp**
3 tbsp	fresh lime juice	**3 tbsp**

Add the penne rigati to 5 litres (8 pints) of boiling water with 1½ teaspoons of salt. Start testing the pasta after 10 minutes and continue to cook until it is *al dente.*

Meanwhile, pour enough water into a saucepan to fill it about 2.5 cm (1 inch) deep. Set a vegetable steamer in the pan and bring the water to the boil. Put the celery in the steamer, cover the pan, and steam the celery until it is tender but still firm – 3 to 4 minutes.

Mash the soft cheese and yogurt together in a bowl with a fork until smooth, then season with the nutmeg, salt and some black pepper. Set the mixture aside.

Heat the oil in a heavy frying pan, add the steamed celery, the shallots and 4 tablespoons of the chopped parsley, and sauté them over medium heat for about 5 minutes, until soft. Drain the pasta and stir it into the celery mixture. Remove the pan from the heat and gently stir the cheese mixture into the pasta and celery. Return the pan to a low heat, cover with a lid and gently warm the pasta mixture through for about 3 minutes. Stir in the lime juice and serve immediately, garnished with the remaining chopped parsley.

Suggested accompaniment: grilled tomatoes or a fresh tomato salad.

Goat Cheese and Parsley Ravioli

Serves 4

Working
(and total)
time: about
1 hour and
15 minutes

Calories
430
Protein
23g
Cholesterol
75mg
Total fat
14g
Saturated fat
2g
Sodium
490mg

175 g	strong plain flour	6 oz
1	egg	1
1	egg white	1
1 tbsp	safflower oil	1 tbsp
175 g	soft goat cheese	6 oz
90 g	fine fresh white breadcrumbs	3 oz
100 g	parsley, finely chopped	3½ oz
45 g	spring onions, finely chopped	1½ oz

	Tomato Sauce	
1 tsp	virgin olive oil	1 tsp
1	small onion, chopped	1
750 g	fresh tomatoes, skinned and roughly chopped	1½ lb
½ tsp	salt	½ tsp
	freshly ground black pepper	

Put the flour in a bowl, add the egg, egg white and oil and stir, gradually mixing in the flour. Transfer to a floured surface and knead for a few minutes. The dough should come cleanly away from the surface. Continue kneading until it is smooth and elastic – about 10 mins. Wrap in plastic film and let it rest for 15 mins.

For the sauce, heat the olive oil in a frying pan over medium heat, sauté the onion for about 3 mins. Add tomatoes, and season. Bring to the boil, cook on high, until the tomatoes soften. Simmer, uncovered, for a further 15 mins. Cool, then purée it. Sieve into a pan and set aside.

To make the filling, combine cheese,

breadcrumbs, 90 g (3 oz) of the parsley and spring onions in a bowl. Divide the dough into 2 portions. Cover one with plastic film. Roll out the other portion on a floured surface into a rectangle measuring about 75 by 15 cm (30 by 6 inches); about 1 mm (¹/₁₆ inch) thick. Form into 18 ravioli, each about 6 by 5 cm (2½ by 2 inches). Repeat with the second portion of dough.

Reheat the tomato sauce over low heat. Add the ravioli to 3 litres (5 pints) of boiling water with 1½ teaspoons of salt. Start testing after 1 minute and cook until they are *al dente*, then drain. Serve immediately with the sauce, and sprinkled with the remaining chopped parsley.

Spaghetti with Omelette and Stir-Fried Vegetables

Serves 6

Working
(and total)
time: about
40 minutes

Calories
290
Protein
13g
Cholesterol
75mg
Total fat
9g
Saturated fat
2g
Sodium
100mg

2	eggs	2
¼ tsp	salt	¼ tsp
¼ tsp	cayenne pepper	¼ tsp
2 tsp	chopped fresh coriander	2 tsp
350 g	dried wholemeal spaghetti	12 oz
2 tbsp	safflower oil	2 tbsp
300 g	bok choy (Chinese chard), washed and dried, stalks removed and julienned, leaves cut into strips	10 oz
2.5 cm	piece fresh ginger root, julienned	1 inch
12	spring onions, white parts only, thinly sliced	12
2	large sweet red peppers, seeded, deribbed and julienned	2
2½ tbsp	low-sodium soy sauce or shoyu	2½ tbsp

Break the eggs into a bowl, add the salt, cayenne pepper and coriander, and whisk well. Pour half the mixture into a hot, lightly oiled non-stick frying pan and cook over medium heat until the underside begins to set – about 1 minute. Carefully lift the edge of the omelette with a spatula and allow any uncooked egg to run underneath; repeat until there is no liquid left on the surface. Flip the omelette over and cook for a further 30 seconds. Slide on to a plate and make the other omelette in the same way. Cool, then slice them into strips.

Cook the pasta in 5 litres (8 pints) of boiling water with 2 teaspoons of salt; start testing it after 10 minutes and cook it until it is al dente. When it is almost ready, heat the oil in a wok or large, heavy frying pan. At 20 second intervals and stirring after each addition, add the bok choy stalks, the ginger, the spring onions together with the red peppers, and finally the bok choy leaves. Drain the pasta thoroughly and add it to the wok together with the omelette strips. Add the soy sauce, stir well and serve.

Suggested accompaniment: a salad of carrot strips and cucumber dressed with a lemon and mint vinaigrette.

Saffron Fettuccine, Hazelnut and Tarragon Sauce

Serves 4

Working time: about 1 hour

Total time: about 1 hour and 15 minutes

Calories 385
Protein 23g
Cholesterol 55mg
Total fat 11g
Saturated fat 2g
Sodium 150mg

175 g	strong plain flour	**6 oz**
60 g	semolina	**2 oz**
¼ tsp	saffron threads, ground with ¼ teaspoon of salt	**¼ tsp**
1	egg	**1**
1 tsp	safflower oil	**1 tsp**
	Hazelnut and Tarragon Sauce	
1 tsp	virgin olive oil	**1 tsp**
1	garlic clove, crushed	**1**

60 g	blanched hazelnuts, toasted and coarsely ground	**2 oz**
250 g	tomatoes, skinned, seeded and chopped	**8 oz**
15 cl	unsalted vegetable stock	**¼ pint**
300 g	low-fat fromage frais	**10 oz**
2 tbsp	chopped fresh tarragon	**2 tbsp**
¼ tsp	salt	**¼ tsp**
	freshly ground black pepper	

Mix the flour, semolina and saffron in a bowl, make a well in the centre. Add the egg, oil and 6 tbsp of water and stir, gradually mixing in the flour. Transfer to a floured surface and knead for a few minutes. The dough should come cleanly away from the surface. Continue kneading the dough until it is smooth and elastic – about 10 minutes. Wrap in plastic film and let it rest for 15 mins.

Heat the oil in a frying pan over medium heat and sauté the garlic until just golden – about 3 mins. Stir in the hazelnuts and tomatoes, and add the stock. Simmer for 2 to 3 mins, then set the pan aside.

Divide the pasta dough into 4 portions. Cover 3 with plastic film. Roll out the fourth portion on a surface sprinkled with semolina, into a sheet about 1 mm (1/16 inch) thick. Cut into 5 mm (¼ inch) wide strips. Roll out the remaining 3 portions and cut them into strips. Add the fettuccine to 3 litres (5 pints) of boiling water with 1½ tsps of salt. Start testing after 1 minute and cook until it is *al dente*. Drain, return to the pan and keep it warm.

Stir the *fromage frais* and tarragon into the sauce, season with the salt and black pepper, return to a low heat and warm through gently. Divide the pasta and top with the sauce.

Tofu and Vegetable Dumpling

Serves 4

Working time:
about
45 minutes

Total time:
about
1 hour

Calories
220

Protein
16g

Cholesterol
0mg

Total fat
8g

Saturated fat
trace

Sodium
235mg

500 g	firm tofu, well drained	**1 lb**
4½ tbsp	cornflour	**4½ tbsp**
1	egg white	**1**
½ tsp	salt	**½ tsp**
60 g	shelled peas, blanched for 1 minute, drained and refreshed under cold running water, or frozen peas, thawed	**2 oz**
60 g	carrots, peeled and very finely diced, blanched for 1 minute,	**2 oz**
	drained and refreshed under cold running water	
6	fresh water chestnuts, peeled and finely diced, or canned water chestnuts, drained and finely diced	**6**
2½ tsp	sesame seeds, toasted	**2½ tsp**
45 cl	unsalted vegetable stock	**¾ pint**
250 g	baby sweetcorn	**8 oz**
250 g	centre leaves of small bok choy	**8 oz**
125 g	mange-tout, strings removed	**4 oz**

Put the tofu in a processor with the cornflour and blend for about 1 minute. In a bowl, whisk the egg white with the salt until it is stiff but not dry. Add the egg white to the tofu, and process briefly to form a smooth paste. Transfer to a bowl, cover, and chill for 30 minutes.

Mix the peas, carrots, chestnuts and 2 teaspoons of the sesame seeds into the tofu paste, divide the mixture into 16 equal portions and mould each into a ball. Bring a saucepan of water to the boil. Line a steamer with muslin and set it over the pan; carefully place the dumplings in a steamer in a single layer. Steam over high heat for 12

minutes, set aside and keep warm.

Meanwhile, bring the vegetable stock to the boil in a saucepan. Add the sweetcorn to the stock, and cook for 3 minutes; add the bok choy leaves and continue to cook for 2 minutes, then add the mange-tout and cook for a further 2 minutes.

Reduce the heat to low and gently lower the dumplings into the stock. Heat them through for about 1 minute. Transfer the dumplings and vegetables to individual plates, sprinkle the remaining sesame seeds over the dumplings, and serve immediately.

Tofu, Courgette and Mushroom Kebabs

Serves 4

Working (and total) time: about 45 minutes

Calories 240

Protein 15g

Cholesterol 0mg

Total fat 15g

Saturated fat 2g

Sodium 100mg

4	courgettes (about 175 g/6 oz each), topped and tailed	4
24	small shallots (about 250 g/8 oz)	24
1	sweet red pepper (about 250 g/8 oz), seeded, deribbed and cut into 2.5 cm (1 inch) squares	1
500 g	firm tofu, well drained, cut into 24 cubes	1 lb
24	small mushrooms (about 500 g/1 lb), wiped clean	24

2 tbsp	virgin olive oil	2 tbsp
	white pepper	
	Olive and Caper Sauce	
4	black olives, stoned and finely chopped	4
1 tbsp	finely chopped capers	1 tbsp
2 tsp	grainy mustard	2 tsp
1 tbsp	finely chopped parsley	1 tbsp
5 tbsp	low-fat plain yogurt	5 tbsp
2 tbsp	fresh lemon or lime juice	2 tbsp

Mix together all the ingredients for the sauce, then set aside to allow the flavours to develop.

Using a canelle knife or the point of a small, sharp knife, remove thin strips of peel lengthwise from each courgette to create a striped effect. Slice the courgettes into 2.5 cm (1 inch) thick rounds. Blanch the courgettes, shallots and pepper squares in boiling water for 2 minutes, refresh them under cold running water, and drain them well. Preheat the grill to high.

Allowing three skewers per serving, thread two each of the courgette rounds, shallots, tofu cubes, mushrooms and pepper squares in turn on to each of 12 skewers. Brush the kebabs with the olive oil and season them with some white pepper.

Place the kebabs under the grill until they are lightly browned – 4 to 6 minutes on each side. Arrange the kebabs on a serving platter and serve the olive and caper sauce separately.

Suggested accompaniment: long-grain rice flavoured with 1 to 2 tablespoons of tomato paste.

Raised Pies with Carrot and Broccoli Filling

Serves 6

Working
time: about
1 hour

Total time:
about
2 hours

Calories
450

Protein
17g

Cholesterol
110mg

Total fat
25g

Saturated fat
6g

Sodium
375mg

500 g	carrots, chopped	1 lb
1	egg, beaten	1
60 g	pine-nuts, ground	2 oz
150 g	low-fat fromage frais	5 oz
¼ tsp	salt	¼ tsp
	freshly ground black pepper	
125 g	broccoli florets	4 oz
½	bunch watercress, stems removed, very finely chopped	½

2 tbsp	skimmed milk, for glazing	2 tbsp
	Hot-Water Crust Pastry	
350 g	wholemeal flour	12 oz
1	egg yolk	1
60 g	polyunsaturated margarine	2 oz
60 g	hard white vegetable fat, diced	2 oz

Steam the carrots for 10 to 20 mins, until tender. Mash roughly. Mix, in a bowl, with the egg, pine-nuts, *fromage frais*, seasoning.

Steam broccoli for 10 mins; chop. Add watercress.

Preheat the oven to 200°C (400°F of Mark 6). Lightly grease six 15 cl (¼ pint) ramekins.

Place the flour in a large bowl. Add the egg yolk. Gently melt the fats with 17.5 cl (6 fl oz) of water in a pan. Increase the heat, and boil. Pour into the flour, stirring to form a soft dough. Knead on a floured surface until smooth; cut off one third. Wrap this in plastic film.

Divide the large piece of dough into 6 equal portions. Roll out each on a floured surface into a circle about 15 cm (6 ins) in diameter. Mould each circle into a ramekin, leaving dough just proud of the rim.

Distribute ½ the carrot mixture among the pastry cases and press it down gently. Top this with the broccoli mixture. Complete the pie fillings with the remaining carrot mixture.

Roll out and cut the reserved dough into 6 circular 'lids' for the pies. Cut a hole in each lid, and glaze with milk. Bake for 40 mins, until crisp. Leave to stand for 3 to 4 mins before unmoulding and serving.

Savoury Pumpkin Pie

Serves 6

Working time: about 30 minutes

Total time: about 1 hour and 15 minutes

Calories 175
Protein 13g
Cholesterol 75mg
Total fat 3g
Saturated fat 1g
Sodium 80mg

500 g	pumpkin or squash, peeled and cut into 1 cm ($\frac{1}{2}$ inch) chunks	**1 lb**
200 g	quark	**7 oz**
2	eggs, beaten	**2**
1	onion, sliced into rings	**1**
1 tsp	safflower oil, plus a little extra for glazing	**1 tsp**
1	garlic clove, crushed	**1**
$\frac{1}{2}$ tsp	ground ginger	**$\frac{1}{2}$ tsp**
$\frac{1}{2}$ tsp	chili powder	**$\frac{1}{2}$ tsp**
$\frac{1}{8}$ tsp	salt	**$\frac{1}{8}$ tsp**
	white pepper	
	Yeast Dough	
175 g	wholemeal flour	**6 oz**
1 tsp	easy-blend dried yeast	**1 tsp**
12.5 cl	skimmed milk	**4 fl oz**

Mix together the flour and yeast in a large bowl. Heat the milk until it is hot to the touch – about 43°C (110°F) – then pour it into the dry ingredients. Knead well for 10 mins, adding a little extra water if necessary, to make a smooth, soft dough. Leave to rest for 10 minutes. Roll out to line a lightly greased 20 cm (8 inch) flan tin.

Preheat the oven to 200°C (400°F or Mark 6).

Steam the pumpkin over a saucepan of boiling water for 10 to 15 minutes, until soft. Transfer to a bowl and mash. When the purée has cooled slightly, beat in the quark and eggs.

Meanwhile, set a quarter of the onion aside and chop the remainder. Heat the oil in a small, heavy-bottomed saucepan over medium heat. Add the chopped onion and garlic, and sauté them for about 3 minutes, until softened but not browned. Stir in the ginger and chili powder.

Transfer the pumpkin mixture to a food processor, and add the contents of the saucepan, the salt and some pepper. Blend the mixture until it is smooth. Pour the filling into the pastry case and level the surface. Press the reserved onion rings lightly into the filling and brush them with the extra safflower oil.

Bake the pie in the oven for 30 to 40 minutes, until it is golden-brown and firm in the centre.

Mustard Cauliflower Flan

Serves 4

Working
time: about
40 minutes

Total time:
about
1 hour and
30 minutes

Calories
330
· Protein
11g
Cholesterol
55mg
Total fat
15g
Saturated fat
4g
Sodium
285mg

1	cauliflower trimmed and divided into small florets (about 350 g/12 oz)	1
1 tsp	virgin olive oil	1 tsp
1	onion, finely chopped	1
1	large cooking apple, peeled, cored and roughly chopped	1
1½ tbsp	Dijon mustard	1½ tbsp
2 tbsp	plain flour	2 tbsp
1	egg, lightly beaten	1

30 cl	skimmed milk	½ pint
¼ tsp	salt	¼ tsp
	white pepper	
	paprika	
	Herb Pastry	
125 g	wholemeal flour	4 oz
60 g	polyunsaturated margarine, chilled	2 oz
2 tbsp	finely chopped fresh coriander	2 tbsp
2 tbsp	finely chopped flat-leaf parsley	2 tbsp

Put the flour in a bowl and rub in the margarine until the mixture resembles fine breadcrumbs. Stir in the herbs. Blend 3 to 4 tbsps of water into the dry ingredients to form a dough. Gather the dough into a ball and knead on a floured surface, until smooth. Roll out to line a flan tin 20 cm (8 ins) in diameter, and about 4 cm (1½ ins) deep. Prick the inside of the pastry case with a fork, and chill for 30 mins.

Preheat the oven to 200°C (400°F or Mark 6). Bake the pastry case for 10 to 15 mins, until crisp. Remove from the oven and reduce the temperature to 180°C (350°F or Mark 4).

Parboil the cauliflower until tender – about

5 mins. Drain, rinse, drain again. Set aside. Heat the oil in a frying pan. Add the onion and fry gently until soft and transparent – about 3 mins. Add the apple and cook for another 4 mins, until the apple is just tender.

Spread the apple mixture inside the flan case and arrange the cauliflower on top. In a bowl, blend the mustard and flour to form a smooth paste. Whisk in the egg, then the milk, a little at a time. Add seasoning and pour into the flan case.

Bake the flan in the oven for 30 to 45 mins, until filling is set. Serve hot or cold, sprinkled with paprika.

Asparagus Strudel

Serves 4

Working
time: about
40 minutes

Total time:
about
1 hour and
10 minutes

Calories
225

Protein
10g

Cholesterol
60mg

Total fat
13g

Saturated fat
5g

Sodium
380mg

350 g	asparagus, trimmed, peeled and sliced diagonally into 5 mm ($\frac{1}{4}$ inch) thick pieces	**12 oz**
175 g	low-fat cheese	**6 oz**
2 tbsp	finely cut chives	**2 tbsp**
2 tbsp	chopped fresh marjoram	**2 tbsp**
1 tbsp	chopped parsley	**1 tbsp**
1	egg, separated	**1**
$\frac{1}{4}$ tsp	salt	**$\frac{1}{4}$ tsp**
	freshly ground black pepper	
5	sheets phyllo pastry, each about 45 by 30 cm (18 by 12 inches)	**5**
30 g	polyunsaturated margarine, melted	**1 oz**
30 g	fresh wholemeal breadcrumbs	**1 oz**

Place the asparagus pieces in a steamer set over a pan of boiling water and steam them for 5 to 6 minutes, until tender. Refresh under cold running water and drain well. Pat the asparagus pieces dry on paper towels.

Put the soft cheese into a bowl with the herbs, egg yolk, salt and some black pepper. Beat the ingredients together well and stir in the drained asparagus. In a clean bowl, whisk the egg white until it is stiff, then fold it carefully into the asparagus mixture using a metal spoon.

Preheat the oven to 200°C (400°F or Mark 6). Lightly grease a baking sheet.

Lay one phyllo sheet flat on the work surface, with a long side towards you. Cover other sheets with a damp cloth to prevent them from drying

out. Brush a little of the margarine over the sheet and sprinkle with one fifth of the breadcrumbs. Lay another sheet on top of the first; brush with margarine and sprinkle it with crumbs in the same way. Repeat with the remaining sheets.

Spoon the asparagus on to the top sheet of phyllo, mounding it in a neat line about 2.5 cm (1 inch) in from the edge nearest to you, and leaving about 2.5 cm (1 inch) clear at each end.

Fold the sides in over the asparagus; loosely roll the pastry up. Place the strudel, with the join underneath, on the baking sheet. Brush the remaining margarine over the top of the pastry.

Bake for 25 to 30 minutes, until golden-brown and puffed up. Serve it either warm or cold, cut into slices.

Broccoli and Pecorino Pasties

Serves 8

Working
time: about
1 hour

Total time:
about
2 hours and
15 minutes

Calories
320

Protein
12g

Cholesterol
60mg

Total fat
13g

Saturated fat
5g

Sodium
150mg

1 tsp	virgin olive oil	1 tsp
1	red onion, finely chopped	1
300 g	purple-sprouting broccoli, divided into florets, stalks and leaves finely chopped	10 oz
100 g	kale, washed, stemmed and chopped	3½ oz
200 g	tomatoes, skinned, seeded and finely chopped	7 oz
¼	fresh hot chili pepper, seeded and finely chopped, or ¼ tsp chili powder	¼

1 tbsp	pine-nuts, toasted	1 tbsp
100 g	low-fat ricotta cheese	3½ oz
45 g	pecorino cheese, finely grated	1½ oz
¼ tsp	salt	¼ tsp
	Lemon Shortcrust Pastry	
400 g	plain flour	14 oz
2 tbsp	virgin olive oil	2 tbsp
30 g	unsalted butter	1 oz
2	eggs, beaten	2
½	lemon, juice only, made up to 14 cl (4½ fl oz) with warm water	½

Sift the flour into a bowl and rub in the oil and butter until the mixture resembles fine breadcrumbs. Pour in ¾ of the eggs, and the diluted lemon juice. Stir, then gather into a ball and knead on a floured surface until smooth. Cover the dough with a tea towel and leave in a cool place for at least 1 hour.

Heat the oil in a pan over low heat. Add the onion, cover, cook until soft and transparent – about 5 mins. Steam the broccoli and kale until no longer tough but still very crisp – about 5 mins. Drain, toss with the onion and leave to

cool a little. Stir in the remaining ingredients.

Divide the dough in half and roll out each on a floured surface into a rectangle 90 by 22 cm (36 by 9 ins). Cut out four 18 to 20 cm (7 to 8 in) circles from each piece.

Preheat the oven to 200°C (400°F or Mark 6).

Place ⅛ of the filling on each round of dough, then fold the rounds over the filling. Pinch the edges together, sealing the filling inside and creating a decorative border. Brush with remaining egg. Bake for 25 mins, until golden. Serve hot.

Spinach and Chinese Cabbage Pie

Serves 6

Working
time: about
30 minutes

Total time:
about
1 hour and
20 minutes

Calories
170
Protein
12g
Cholesterol
90mg
Total fat
10g
Saturated fat
5g
Sodium
430mg

500 g	Chinese cabbage, leaves separated and washed	**1 lb**
500 g	Spinach, washed, stems removed	**1 lb**
2	eggs	**2**
1	egg white	**1**
175 g	low-fat cottage cheese	**6 oz**
3 tbsp	cut chives	**3 tbsp**
2 tbsp	chopped fresh marjoram	**2 tbsp**
¼ tsp	salt	**¼ tsp**
	freshly ground black pepper	
6	sheets phyllo pastry, each about 45 by 30 cm (18 by 12 inches)	**6**
45 g	unsalted butter, melted	**1½ oz**

Bring a large saucepan of water to the boil, add Chinese cabbage leaves and cook for 1 min, until they wilt. Lift the leaves out of the water into a colander and drain well. Blanch the spinach in the same water for 1 min, then pour into a colander and refresh under cold running water. Squeeze the spinach dry in muslin. Roughly chop both vegetables.

Put the eggs and egg white into a large bowl and whisk lightly. Add the chopped Chinese cabbage and spinach, the cottage cheese, chives, marjoram, salt and some black pepper. Mix well. Set aside, while you prepare the phyllo pastry. Preheat the oven to 190°C (375°F or Mark 5).

Grease a 30 by 22 cm (12 by 9 inch) oven dish. Cut the sheets of phyllo pastry in half crosswise. Place one piece of phyllo in the bottom of the prepared dish and brush it with a little of the melted butter. Add another three pieces of phyllo, brushing each one lightly with melted butter. Pour the Chinese cabbage and spinach into the dish and level the surface. Cover the filling with the remaining eight pieces of phyllo pastry, brushing each piece with melted butter as before. Using a small sharp knife, mark the top layer of phyllo with a diamond pattern.

Put the pie in the oven and bake it for 50 to 55 minutes, until the top is golden-brown.

Baguette and Brie Bake

Serves 4

Working
time: about
10 minutes

Total time:
about
40 minutes

Calories
220

Protein
14g

Cholesterol
80mg

Total fat
8g

Saturated fat
1g

Sodium
460mg

100 g	Brie or Camembert cheese, chilled	3½ oz
1	small baguette (about 175 g/6 oz)	1
1	egg	1

2	egg whites	2
20 cl	semi-skimmed milk	7 fl oz
	freshly ground black pepper	

Preheat the oven to 180°C (350°F or Mark 4). Lightly grease a large, shallow ovenproof dish.

Using a sharp knife, slice the cheese lengthwise into 5 mm (¼ inch) thick slices, then cut each slice into pieces about 3 cm (1¼ inch) wide, to give 16 small slices. Cut the baguette into 16 slices.

Fit the slices of bread and cheese alternately into the prepared dish. Beat the egg and egg whites in a bowl, add the milk and some black pepper, then carefully pour the mixture over the bread and cheese, ensuring that all the bread is thoroughly soaked.

Place the dish in the oven and bake for 30 minutes, until the surface is golden-brown and crisp, and the custard is just firm in the centre. Serve at once.

Suggested accompaniments: salad of mixed leaves; tomato, cucumber and onion salad.

Scorzonera and Asparagus Muffins

Serves 4

Working
(and total)
time: about
30 minutes

Calories
240
Protein
20g
Cholesterol
20mg
Total fat
7g
Saturated fat
4g
Sodium
520mg

4	scorzonera (about 250 g/8 oz), topped, tailed and scrubbed well	4
12	asparagus spears, trimmed and peeled	12
4	wholemeal muffins, halved horizontally	4
4 tsp	low-fat fromage frais freshly ground black pepper	4 tsp

1 tbsp	finely chopped mixed fresh herbs (tarragon, chervil, dill, parsley)	1 tbsp
125 g	low-fat mozzarella cheese, thinly sliced	4 oz
1 tsp	paprika	1 tsp
2 tsp	finely cut chives	2 tsp

Cook the scorzonera in a saucepan of lightly boiling water, covered, for 10 to 15 minutes, until it is tender when pierced with a sharp knife. Drain the scorzonera and, using the back of a knife, scrape each root gently under cold running water until all the black skin has been removed. Cut each scorzonera root into three pieces of equal length.

Meanwhile, steam the asparagus in a steamer basket over a pan of gently simmering water for about 10 minutes, until it is tender but still crisp. Remove the asparagus from the steamer and place the spears on paper towels to dry.

Preheat the grill to medium. Toast the muffins on their uncut side only. Spread the untoasted side of the warm muffins with the *fromage frais*, and season them with some black pepper and the chopped mixed fresh herbs. Put three asparagus spears on each of four of the halves, and three pieces of scorzonera on each of the other four halves. Lay the mozzarella slices on top of the vegetables. Place the muffins under the grill until the mozzarella has melted and is begining to bubble and brown slightly – 3 to 5 minutes. Garnish the scorzonera muffins with the paprika and the asparagus muffins with the chives. Serve at once.

Italian Poor Man's Salad

Serves 4

Working time: about 30 minutes

Total time: about 2 hours and 30 minutes (includes chilling)

Calories 245

Protein 10g

Cholesterol 0mg

Total fat 10g

Saturated fat 1g

Sodium 255mg

125 g	slightly stale wholemeal bread, crusts removed	**4 oz**
125 g	slightly stale black rye bread, crusts removed	**4 oz**
250 g	ripe tomatoes, skinned, seeded and diced, seeds and juice reserved canned or bottled tomato juice (optional)	**8 oz**
4	small black olives, stoned and finely chopped	**4**
125 g	cucumber, cut into 2.5 cm (1 inch) long bâtonnets	**4 oz**

4	small green olives, stoned and finely chopped	**4**
6	large basil leaves, shredded	**6**
6	large rocket leaves, shredded	**6**
1 tbsp	chopped fresh chervil leaves	**1 tbsp**
1 tbsp	finely chopped fresh tarragon	**1 tbsp**
1 tbsp	finely chopped flat-leaf parsley	**1 tbsp**
2 tbsp	virgin olive oil	**2 tbsp**
2 tbsp	white wine	**2 tbsp**
3tbsp	red wine	**3 tbsp**
	freshly ground black pepper basil sprigs, for garnish	

Grate the wholemeal and rye bread to make breadcrumbs, placing the two in separate bowls. Sieve the seeds and juice from the tomatoes. This should yield about 10 cl (3½ fl oz); make up the quantity with canned/bottled tomato juice, if necessary. Divide between the 2 bowls and mix well.

Add the tomatoes and black olives to the wholemeal breadcrumbs, and the cucumber and green olives to the rye breadcrumbs. Divide the basil, rocket, chervil, tarragon and parsley equally between the 2 bowls. Pour 1 tbsp of oil into each bowl and mix well. Finally, add as much wine as the mixture in each bowl will absorb, using the white wine with the wholemeal breadcrumbs and the red wine with the rye breadcrumbs. Season each bowl with pepper. Cover the bowls with damp cloths and place in the refrigerator for 2 hours.

Serve the bread salads cool or chilled, garnished with basil sprigs.

Bread, Cheese and Onion Pudding

Serves 8			Calories 300	
Working time: about 40 minutes			Protein 12g	
			Cholesterol 60mg	
Total time: about 2 hours and 30 minutes			Total fat 14g	
			Saturated fat 4g	
			Sodium 485mg	

75 g	polyunsaturated margarine	**2½ oz**		**2**	eggs	**2**
2	large onions, thinly sliced	**2**		**2**	egg whites	**2**
500 g	courgettes, julienned	**1 lb**		**60 cl**	skimmed milk	**1 pint**
2 tsp	Dijon mustard	**2 tsp**			freshly ground black pepper	
2	garlic cloves, crushed	**2**		**90 g**	Cheddar cheese, grated	**3 oz**
24	thin slices white bread, remove crusts	**24**				

Heat 15 g (½ oz) of the margarine in a large, non-stick frying pan over medium heat. Add the onions and cook them gently for about 5 minutes, until they are soft but not brown. Add the courgette julienne and cook for another 6 minutes, stirring occasionally. Remove the pan from the heat and allow the courgettes and onions to cool for about 15 minutes.

Meanwhile, put the remaining 60 g (2 oz) of margarine in a bowl with the mustard and garlic, and blend together until smooth. Spread thinly over the bread. Cut each slice into four triangles.

Put the eggs, egg whites and milk into a mixing bowl, add some black pepper, and whisk the eggs and milk together lightly.

Grease a 30 by 22 cm (12 by 9 inch) ovenproof dish. Place one third of the bread triangles in a layer in the bottom of the dish, and spread half of the onion and courgette mixture over the top. Sprinkle on one third the grated cheese. Add another third of the bread triangles, the remaining onion and courgette mixture, and another third of the cheese. Arrange the remaining triangles of bread decoratively on the top, overlapping them slightly. Pour the whisked eggs and milk over the bread. Scatter the remaining grated cheese evenly over the top. Set the pudding aside in a cool place for 1 hour, to allow the bread to soften and soak up the eggs and milk.

Preheat the oven to 190°C (375°F or Mark 5). Cook for 45 to 50 minutes, until well puffed up, set and golden-brown. Serve immediately.

Burghul-Stuffed Phyllo Packages

Serves 4

Working time: about 35 minutes

Total time: about 1 hour and 45 minutes (includes soaking)

Calories 315
Protein 10g
Cholesterol 0mg
Total fat 10g
Saturated fat 2g
Sodium 115mg

125 g	burghul, soaked in 60 cl (1 pint) hot water for 1 hour	**4 oz**
175 g	carrots, grated	**6 oz**
6	dried apricots, chopped	**6**
1 tbsp	currants	**1 tbsp**
60 g	unsalted cashew nuts, coarsely chopped, or pine-nuts	**2 oz**
½ tsp	ground cumin	**½ tsp**
½ tsp	ground coriander	**½ tsp**
2 tbsp	finely chopped parsley	**2 tbsp**
⅛ tsp	salt	**⅛ tsp**
	freshly ground black pepper	
5	sheets phyllo pastry, each about 45 by 30 cm (18 by 12 inches)	**5**
2 tsp	safflower oil	**2 tsp**

Preheat the oven to 200°C (400°F or Mark 6). Lightly grease a baking sheet.

Drain the burghul well, pressing out as much moisture as possible. Place the burghul in a large bowl and add the carrots, apricots, currants, cashew nuts, cumin, coriander, parsley, salt and some black pepper. Mix thoroughly.

Lay out one sheet of phyllo pastry on the work surface; keep the other sheets covered by a clean, damp cloth while you work, to prevent them from drying out.. Brush a little oil over the sheet on the work surface. Place a quarter of the burghul mixture near one end of the sheet, half

way between the two longer sides, and flatten it down gently. Fold the shorter edge of the pastry over the filling, fold in the two longer side edges, then roll the stuffed section up to the other end, to form a package. Place the package on the baking sheet, with the join underneath. Roll up another three phyllo packages in the same way.

Cut the remaining sheet of pastry into strips. Crumple the strips loosely in your hand, and use some to decorate the top of each package. Brush the remaining oil or a little skimmed milk over the packages, and bake them in the oven for 20 to 25 minutes, until they are golden-brown.

Useful weights and measures

Weight Equivalents

Avoirdupois		*Metric*
1 ounce	=	28.35 grams
1 pound	=	254.6 grams
2.3 pounds	=	1 kilogram

Liquid Measurements

$1/4$ pint	=	$1 1/2$ decilitres
$1/2$ pint	=	$1/4$ litre
scant 1 pint	=	$1/2$ litre
$1 3/4$ pints	=	1 litre
1 gallon	=	4.5 litres

Liquid Measures

1 pint	= 20 fl oz	= 32 tablespoons
$1/2$ pint	= 10 fl oz	= 16 tablespoons
$1/4$ pint	= 5 fl oz	= 8 tablespoons
$1/8$ pint	= $2 1/2$ fl oz	= 4 tablespoons
$1/16$ pint	= $1 1/4$ fl oz	= 2 tablespoons

Solid Measures

1 oz almonds, ground = $3 3/4$ level tablespoons
1 oz breadcrumbs fresh = 7 level tablespoons
1 oz butter, lard = 2 level tablespoons
1 oz cheese, grated = $3 1/2$ level tablespoons
1 oz cocoa = $2 3/4$ level tablespoons
1 oz desiccated coconut = $4 1/2$ tablespoons
1 oz cornflour = $2 1/2$ tablespoons
1 oz custard powder = $2 1/2$ tablespoons
1 oz curry powder and spices = 5 tablespoons
1 oz flour = 2 level tablespoons
1 oz rice, uncooked = $1 1/2$ tablespoons
1 oz sugar, caster and granulated = 2 tablespoons
1 oz icing sugar = $2 1/2$ tablespoons
1 oz yeast, granulated = 1 level tablespoon

American Measures

16 fl oz	=1 American pint
8 fl oz	=1 American standard cup
0.50 fl oz	=1 American tablespoon

(*slightly smaller than British Standards Institute tablespoon*)

0.16 fl oz	=1 American teaspoon

Australian Cup Measures
(*Using the 8-liquid-ounce cup measure*)

1 cup flour	4 oz
1 cup sugar (crystal or caster)	8 oz
1 cup icing sugar (free from lumps)	5 oz
1 cup shortening (butter, margarine)	8 oz
1 cup brown sugar (lightly packed)	4 oz
1 cup soft breadcrumbs	2 oz
1 cup dry breadcrumbs	3 oz
1 cup rice (uncooked)	6 oz
1 cup rice (cooked)	5 oz
1 cup mixed fruit	4 oz
1 cup grated cheese	4 oz
1 cup nuts (chopped)	4 oz
1 cup coconut	$2 1/2$ oz

Australian Spoon Measures

	level tablespoon
1 oz flour	2
1 oz sugar	$1 1/2$
1 oz icing sugar	2
1 oz shortening	1
1 oz honey	1
1 oz gelatine	2
1 oz cocoa	3
1 oz cornflour	$2 1/2$
1 oz custard powder	$2 1/2$

Australian Liquid Measures
(*Using 8-liquid-ounce cup*)

1 cup liquid	8 oz
$2 1/2$ cups liquid	20 oz (1 pint)
2 tablespoons liquid	1 oz
1 gill liquid	5 oz ($1/4$ pint)